STO

8-5-76

A Social History of

LOYD
GROSSMAN

A Social History of

ROCK
MUSIC

FROM THE GREASERS TO GLITTER ROCK

DAVID McKAY COMPANY, INC.
NEW YORK

Library of Congress Cataloging in Publication Data

Grossman, Loyd, 1950–
  A social history of rock music.

  Includes index.
  1. Rock music—United States—History and criticism.
  2. Rock music—Great Britain—History and criticism.
  3. United States—Popular culture. 4. Great Britain—
  Popular culture. I. Title.
  ML3561.R62G76   301.5′8   76–10261
  ISBN 0–679–50610–1

MANUFACTURED IN THE UNITED STATES OF AMERICA

Designed by Bob Antler

CONTENTS

Preface   *vii*

1. *BEFORE THE FLOOD (1954–1963)*   *3*
    Media Mechanics, 3
    The Anatomy of Pop Songs and High and Low
        Culture, 10
    Why Bother?, 15
    Good Old Rock and Roll: Teen Culture in the
        Eisenhower Era, 16
    The Golden Age of Rock and Roll?, 21
    Technoculting Sputnik and Cold War Action,
        24

2. *THE COMING OF THE NEW ROCK*
    (1964–1966)   *31*
    The Beatles and the British Invasion, 31
    Pop Style and the Fashion Renascence, 39
    Hair and History, 44
    Decadancing in the Night—The Rolling Stones,
        46
    The British Ascendancy, 51

CONTENTS

3. **THE AMERICAN REACTION
(1965–1967)**   61
Ghosts of the Hootenanny Era, 61
Horrors, It's Art!, 64
No More Surfin', 67
Psychedelic Madness, 70
The Noble Savage, 73
Woodstock Nation Sells Out, 75

4. **ROCK AT ITS ZENITH (1967–1972)**   83
The New Transatlantic Style, 83
Baroque and Roll, 90

5. **ROCK-AND-ROLL FACTS,
MYTHS, AND LEGENDS**   105
The Stars and Their System, 105
The Rock Establishment, 110
Women in Rock, 117
Rock and Roll Technology, 121

6. **NEW THRILLS FOR
THE JADED GENERATION
(1972–1975)**   131

7. **NEAR THE END OF
THE TRAIL:
THE LEVI-ING OF AMERICA**   141

Index   145

PREFACE

I dislike prefaces that are long apologies for the short-comings of both book and author. In this case I know that we both have our faults, but it is up to the reader to find them and criticize accordingly. I will only offer a few clues as to what those faults may be. I have made no effort to be comprehensive, objective, and definitive. Other books have attempted to provide exhaustive, well-documented, dispassionate histories of rock and roll. A few have succeeded, most have not. In general, such attempts to make rock music a subject of pseudo-academic inquiry have only served to make the music and the culture that goes with it appear boring and lifeless. In the present volume I have tried to set down only what I believe has been important in the development of rock and roll in the last two decades and to describe its real place in the social scheme of things. I hope that readers find the story entertaining and interesting.

I must reverse the traditional author's disclaimer about friends not being responsible for whatever faults a book may have. In my case my friends have been only too tolerant and encouraging. Perhaps they thought that I would never get around to writing down all the ideas that I have expressed about rock music!

Without the enthusiasm, nagging, and encouragement of a number of people this book would not have been written. J.P. Donlon, rock critic turned fashion editor, was responsible for prodding me toward my publisher, and Sandi Gelles-Cole's early involvement was a great help in getting this project started.

A number of people who are in the "rock business" have wittingly and unwittingly been sources of feedback and information: Marshall Chess, Frank Modica, Fred Mancuso, Derek Taylor, and Tony Smith. Thanks also to George Melly and Ian Whitcomb for their books and pop-culture knowledge.

Three great friends, who happen to be professionally involved with rock and roll, have been ideological sparring partners, guiding lights, and sources of both good and indifferent jokes: Geoff Haslam, record producer and occasional bass player extraordinaire; Ed Goodgold, rock and roll's leading Talmudic authority; and Johnny Stirling, whose consideration, thoughtfulness, and generosity are equaled only by his inability to mix a proper Bloody Mary.

Bob Somma has been a dedicated friend, a tolerant former editor at *Fusion,* and a ferocious tennis opponent.

Thanks to Willie and Veronica Peel, at whose home a large part of this book was written, for their friendship and interest. I am most grateful to those who provided room, typewriters, and other amenities at various times while this book was being written: Geoff and Julia Haslam, London; Johnny and Susan Stirling, London; Mr. and Mrs. E.C. Haslam, the Green Farm, Wark-on-Tyne; Col. and Mrs. W.J. Stirling of Keir, Dunblane.

A special note of thanks to Philippe and Vivienne Halban, whose toleration, benignity, and unflagging good humor made the final revision of this book immeasurably less difficult.

A few women, who shall be unnamed, were important sources of inspiration and irritation.

"Well done" to the manufacturers of Grape Nuts, Cott Diet Chocolate Mint Soda and Olympia typewriters.

My brother, Neal, has been an indefatigable provider of good advice and assistance.

Lastly, my greatest debt is to my parents, to whom this book is dedicated in love and admiration.

Headington,
Oxford
1975

BEFORE THE FLOOD
1954-1963

● ● ●
MEDIA MECHANICS
● ● ●

It may be a cliché to say that all the distinguishing factors of the rock-and-roll cosmos were forged in the crucible of the nineteen fifties, but, like most clichés, there is more than a modicum of truth in it. I don't propose to discuss the fifties at any great length; my experience of that decade was shaped by the exigencies of childhood, so that during even the most momentous of political or cultural occurrences I was too preoccupied with learning long division or agonizing over lost milk money to experience the major events of those years. Fragments of the culture did, however, obtrude upon my life sufficiently for me to have memories of the Everly brothers on the Ed Sullivan Show, peg pants,

Calypso, white socks, and various other weird and terrible shibboleths of nineteen-fifties American culture. Suffice it to say that the fifties were pretty abysmal years—repressed, alienated, smug, and generally "uptight."

The economic expansion and material abundance of the decade was undeniable, though, as General Motors, General Electric, and the other members of the industrial high command armed the men and women of America with the weapons of conquest in the battle for domestic cleanliness, psychic satisfaction, and suburban status: washing machines, lawn mowers, ice crushers, electric blenders, and television sets littered the playrooms, kitchens, and greenswards of America in unprecedented profusion.

Significant for the pop culture of the next decade, the fifties was a spiritual golden age for the new tools of twentieth-century mass culture: television, and the hi-fi phonograph. For a time the United States was obsessed with these new means of communication and entertainment, indeed more obsessed with the machinery than with the entertainment which the machinery so obligingly dispensed. Of course the fifties was an era in the thrall of technological novelty, and the American people have always had an inordinate enthusiasm for gadgetry of all sorts; even today I suspect that most people get at least a tiny thrill when they switch on the latest electric appliance and—woweezowee—it works!

Television does not really bear directly on the history of pop music. Yet television is an exemplary modern entertainment medium and even though much vaunted, denigrated, and analyzed, it is worth a few words here because of the immense role it plays in shaping the modern American public's attitude toward and response to culture.

Television is a one-cost, low-operating-expense medium for the culture consumer. After the somewhat high initial purchase price, viewing is free. A viewer can watch television for as many hours a day as he wishes until the set or his brain burns out. A large amount of programming is available, and though much of it is drearily familiar, the illusion of choice—which is much less taxing than real choice—is there as well as the drawing-room power trip of direct and instantaneous control over the medium. If the viewer doesn't like what he's got on the screen, he can switch channels or turn off the set—both less costly and embarrassing than walking out of a cinema or a theater in the midst of a show.

Most significantly, television is the most effortless and enveloping of communications media: it creates an almost stifling environment of languor and passivity. The habitual viewer may be like a starving man lost in the jungle—somnolent, plodding, alienated from the world. The world on the television screen is rarely urgent or compelling; it is only the most fantasmic simulacrum of the world. Yet the syrupy simplicity of the televised world is so seductive and pervasive and insinuates itself so thoroughly into the mind of the viewer that the entire world becomes televisionized.

Although the inextricable mixing of commercial announcements (broadcast euphemism for advertising) with programming is a prominent feature of both newspapers and commercial radio, in television the similarity between advertising and programs is more marked, especially when one notes that television commercials are often more elaborately produced than television programs. While commercials are ostensibly a way to pay for programming, more often than not programming appears to be mere filling between commercials. Apparently it was thought that people would not buy and turn on television sets in order to watch commercial after commercial. This hopeful appraisal of public sensibilities should not blind us to the fact that from the beginning of commercial television, much programming (particularly melodramas and situation comedies) has provided a model of daily life in which the same variety of human-to-human and human-to-product relationships which are at the heart of commercials are enacted. While it is undeniably important to smell good, have white teeth, and not enter Dad's study without knocking, the ceaseless homilies of television programs are so tangled into a mare's nest of exhortations to buy some of the most worthless and degrading products imaginable that even the most basic social virtues cannot be represented to television viewers without being set into an ethos of crass and distorted standards of value.

The indirect social costs of television can be high: for the privilege of being able to view any number of similar programs of what in most cases can only loosely be called entertainment, the viewer must endure a large number of commercials, must allow the quality of the programs he watches to be debauched by the demands of commercialism, and must suffer a diminution of his critical faculties—that is, if he had any to begin with. This portrait of a nation peopled by a legion of zombies programmed to listlessly yesma'am and yessir and filled with the desire to purchase the latest brand of toilet-bowl disinfectant or marshmallow-coated breakfast cereal or whatever other high-profit refuse is being pushed by the captains of industry may be extreme, but it is the end to which a nation crazed and enslaved by television, as the United States has seemed to be at times, may come. Similarly many of the nation's recent difficulties are related to the ease with which TV may be used to persuade people to mindlessly endorse specious political programs and to vote for attractive but malefic political candidates.

To all the above comments must be added the proviso and confession that, of course, not all television is bad, that I watch and enjoy television, that there are good and even outstanding programs on television, that television can be entertaining and edifying, that blah, blah, blah, but any analysis of television must recognize that as television became a more prominent and permanent feature of American life there was a dulling effect on the national sensibilities, if only because the mass audience and great expense of television militate against both easy access to the medium by all but large and powerful groups and the presentation of unorthodox or arcane subjects. Television tends to be aesthetically and philosophically monolithic.

The improvement and proliferation of records and phonographs have less sinister though equally commercial implications. From the late forties and throughout the fifties improvements in the format of recorded music and in the technology of sound recording and reproduction led to advances in the quality of records and record players available to the public. Following their introduction in the late forties, LPs or albums began to dominate the record market, although they were not to reach their zenith until the sixties and seventies. Albums and the new 45-r.p.m. singles, which replaced the more cumbersome and fragile 78-r.p.m. discs, offered a better quality sound, increased durability, and greater ease of storage and handling than their predecessors. The LP (short for long playing), as its name indicates, contained more recorded material—usually the equivalent of six singles (which are really doubles)—about forty to forty-five minutes' worth of music, and this additional time was to influence the length and complexity of pop compositions in the coming decades.

Contemporaneous with the change in format from the 78 to the album and the 45 single were the development of the hi-fi (high fidelity) phonograph and various advances in recording technology. The hi-fi, which in retrospect sounds remarkably lo-fi, provided a more natural sound than any previous phonograph, and the shift to recording on magnetic tape rather than by the older electro-mechanical methods produced better recorded sound and gave performers and record producers (more about them later, but for now we can say that their role combines that of the movie producer and director) a new arsenal of acoustical gimmickry, such as editing and double-tracking, with which to work.

Records offer the same sort of individual control over the medium of entertainment as does television. It has been noted that once one has purchased a particular record, one can in effect command the entertainer to perform the selection over and over again by playing the record as many times as one wishes. To this must be added the ability to control the tone—the amount of bass and treble—and the volume of the performance, things which are impossible in the concert hall, where the performer and the acoustical properties of the hall are in command. The ability to turn the control knobs on a phonograph as one chooses may not seem like much of a sop to whatever will to dominate exists in most people, but at a time in history when individual impuissance is felt in most human activity, even the small victory of being able to say, "Paul McCartney, I am going to make you sing 'Yesterday' in a grating trebly voice at deafening volume for the next three hours" can be pretty significant.

While the elements of command and control are similar to television, the economics and effects of listening to records are quite different. Listening to records requires a considerable and ongoing financial outlay, for phonographs must be purchased and replaced or improved as sound reproduction technology develops. In addition, one must constantly be purchasing the latest releases—remember that we're talking about the pop music world, where permanence is a vice, novelty a virtue.

Generally the listener chooses which of the new recordings he or she will purchase by listening to them on radio stations which play pop music, by hearing about "good" records from friends, by automatically buying the latest recordings of favorite performers, or perhaps by reading reviews of records in newspapers and magazines. Because the listener must pay for the privilege of listening, listening becomes more selective and hence more thoughtful and literate than watching television. A listener may be able to talk at some length about why he or she likes a particular record and while much of what is said may be the most awful nonsense, the point is that television viewers don't often critically discuss what they watch, while record listeners almost invariably discuss what they listen to.

This may be an appropriate point to mention the place of radio in the pop-culture scheme. On the eve of World War II radio was the most important entertainment medium, but in the following decades it was largely superseded by the more spectacular (television) or the more sophisticated and selective (records) media. Increasingly radio programming relied upon recorded rather than "live" music, and for the purposes of our discussion radio is most important as a medium for the airing of new records and as a tool for spreading news of "what's happening" in certain areas of pop culture. That is, radio is more important as a marketing device for pop records than as a significant influence on the aesthetic operating principles of pop music, so it will only concern us tangentially.

• • •

THE ANATOMY OF POP SONGS AND HIGH AND LOW CULTURE

• • •

Listening to records requires considerable involvement and participation on the part of the listener, for recorded music does not create the same suffocating totality of environment as television unless the entertainee wills it. When someone chooses to listen to records seriously, not just as ambient noise on the car radio to relieve road tedium or to accompany covert humping in suburban cul-de-sacs, he must become actively involved in the music process, which is why at any given moment in our great land there must be an army of teen-agers frantically boogalooing to their favorite records in the privacy of their rooms. We might note the beat-crazed-teen-ager-with-transistor-radio-glued-to-ear-caterwauling-lyrics-of-favorite-record-being-played as an image which became a sort of icon of pop-music culture in America. Listener participation—this includes foot tapping, writhing, clapping, and trying to sing along—is a vital part of the pop-music process. A pop song belongs to the listener not just because he has purchased the disc or bought the products he hears advertised on his favorite radio station, but because the listener involves himself with the song and completes it. A pop song can't exist without its audience, for a pop song without an audience is like a mirror without someone to look into it.

All of which brings us to the difficult task of defining what a pop song is. A pop song is a commercial production. A person writes a pop song not only to express himself but also in the hope that it will sell. Unlike folk songs, which are meant to be musical statements about the everyday life or perhaps the mythology of book-dumb but reputedly life-smart hayseeds, the pop song, while often just as telling a comment about life as the folk song, is also a way to make a living. Folk songs are written to lighten the burden of work in the fields, to ease the monotony of machine tending, to celebrate or commemorate an event. They are composed and performed by nonprofessionals for nonprofessionals; they are the common property of common folk. In contrast the pop song is destined from birth for the marketplace.

A pop song must make as incisive or exemplary a statement about life as a folk song, but the pop song does it to sell, while the folk song does it to exist. In a pop song the subject matter may be incidental to the commercial motive and so secondary to the mode of presentation or the manner of marketing. This emphasis on the commerciality of the pop song is in no way meant to be pejorative; it is merely to point out that in the pop world commercial considerations loom large. A pop songwriter may decide to write trenchantly about the repression of teen-agers or touchingly about young love, or with less poetic motivation he may decide to write about a boy who knocks up his girl friend and commits suicide by driving his Studebaker into a freight train, because he thinks that such a juicy topic might sell to the kids in Smallville.

What the kids in Smallville or Topeka or San Diego will or will not buy and why they will or will not buy is at the heart of the pop-music mechanism and indeed at the heart of all mass commercial art.

Pop music is, after all, a mass commercial art. Pop is short for popular and so concerned neither with pleasing a few wealthy patrons who collect Meissen and drink cognac nor with tickling the rarified senses of a cadre of mincing aesthetes. The shakers and movers of pop music do battle daily for the disposable income if not truly the affections of the mass, the rabble, the big crowd, the mob, the dregs, hoi polloi, or whatever one cares to call us.

While the average man or woman in the street may be a paragon of civic virtue, familial devotion, kindness to animals, and all the other qualities which civilization deems good and beautiful, one might say that in the aggregate people just don't have very good taste. Because the consumers of mass art don't have good taste, mass art operates within its own parameters of taste and with its own matrix of goods and no-goods. That most mass art is in bad taste or just plain no good is quite irrelevant, as is the fact that some mass art is quite good —often much better than the "real art" favored by high culture—because in the world of mass art the most important standards are monetary success and "I don't know much about art, but I know what I like."

"I don't know much about art, but I know what I like" can be dangerous because it is rarely the product of long or deep reflection; it is rather a purely formulaic and quite mechanical endorsement of current mass favorites and an apology for ignorance couched as an assertion of taste and aesthetic independence. "I don't know much about art, but I know what I like" means "I don't know much about most things, but I know what

I don't like." Given this canon of taste and the fact that most consumers of mass art are for various reasons—sloth, haste, ignorance and other sins and quasi-sins—not prone to reflect on the art which they consume, it is hardly surprising that mass art and the media that distribute it should have a great deal of aboveness: that control, and hence taste, should emanate from the manufacturers and distributors who, sensing that the public doesn't know what it wants but knows what it doesn't want, strive to maintain and secure their places in the commercial sun by promoting the production and distribution of art which is innocuous, anodyne and, because inoffensive to everyone, profitable.

These, then, are the features of mass art. First, because mass art must be an interpretation of reality which is acceptable to a mass of undiscriminating consumers, it must be conventional and undemanding. Second, standards of taste in mass art are formulated more by the producers than by the consumers. Third, mass art reinforces and defends its own aesthetic mode until it is clearly demonstrated that a new artistic mode can be equally lucrative, at which time a wholesale and almost indecently hasty conversion to the new mode of mass artistic expression takes place. Mass art tends to progress by fits and starts rather than by organic evolution.

What are some of the manifestations of mass art? In architecture, the ranch house and the World Trade Center; in furniture, the fur-covered Mediterranean-style waterbed and the Barcalounger; in food, the Big Mac; in sculpture, the Hummel figurine; in visual art, paintings on velvet of wide-eyed waifs; and in music, but of course, the pop song.

Apart from those qualities which it shares with the rest of mass art, the pop song has certain unique traits.

It must be a fairly brief composition because in order to sell a work of art to the mass audience it must be easily comprehensible, that is, technically simple and not inordinately long. This tendency is reinforced by the technical and economic requirements of pop music's principal marketing medium—radio, which plays 45-r.p.m. singles. Pop songs are usually three to five minutes long because that is the amount of recorded material that can best be carried on one side of a single, because radio is an important showcase of new pop songs and the short format allows a greater number of songs to be played each hour as well as for the more frequent insertion of commercials, and because in general a number of short bits of entertainment allows for more flexibility in programming.

But the most outstanding characteristic of the pop song is the way it combines art and commerce. The very existence of a pop song is predicated on its commercial success, for the pop song realizes its aesthetic in the marketplace. By trying to answer an earlier question—"Will the kids in Smallville buy it?" or, as many a record industry executive has asked, "Sure it's good, but will it sell?"—we may come to the essence of pop music. But this leads to a most intriguing question: What makes a pop song sell?

Any of a number of things may make a pop song sell: catchy, nonsensical words ("Ta Ra Ra Boomdeay" was the first "smash hit" of modern, i.e., post-1880, pop music); a strong, simple beat or rhythmic novelty (one, two, cha-cha-cha); cheap sentimentality; the telling of a story; a clear or clever statement about some facet of everyday life; a pleasant melody; performance by an endearing entertainer—any of these things may make a pop song a hit, a song that many people want to listen to and buy.

A pop song, like a streetwalker, must display its attractions quite shamelessly, since most have the same basic equipment. Pop songs must make themselves remembered by the listener after he or she has heard them only a few times, usually under less than ideal conditions on the radio amidst a slew of similar songs. Within each song there is the same relentless hammering away at the most commercial element, whether it be a musical figure, a catchword or phrase, or the continual repeats of a hummable chorus. The pop song is a bit of caricature, a song with quite ridiculously exaggerated features. As self-advertisement it is superb and it must be to survive. While the great musical classics appear to us as herald angels giving us a glimpse of some transcendental beyond, pop songs attach themselves to us like barnacles delivering today's newspapers. Of course not all pop songs make it and become hits, and what is hideous is that they all try so hard.

● ● ●
WHY BOTHER?
● ● ●

Taking all the above into account and recognizing that pop music is mass consumable, crassly commercial, exploitive, ephemeral, and so on, one might easily ask: Why should any reasonable and intelligent person, as anyone who reads or writes a book fancies himself to be, waste time thinking about pop songs? The immediate answer is that good pop songs are good to listen to. The deeper answer is that the very best pop songs incisively and compactly give us a picture of the way the world works, or seems to work, at our time in history. The world view of the pop song is presented with such a sense of urgency and so intense a "hey listen to me" that pop songs as pieces of art have a viscerality and impact that other, more explicitly "artistic," forms of expression often lack. Rock and roll in particular is worth our consideration, for its rise to the dominance of the pop music world is something of a triumph. For all its failings and excesses, rock and roll is a more democratic and authentic musical expression than the june-moon-spooning of Tin Pan Alley.

Pop music makes no effort to be timeless, perfect, and classical; when it does it runs off the rails. The culture buffs of the future will listen to Beatles' records not as we listen to Mozart, but rather to find out what sort of life our generation led. Pop music is an expression—perhaps "symptom" might be a better word—of our culture and at the same time an influence on the way we live and think about our lives. Above all pop music is made by us and for us, and knowing something about it helps us to know ourselves better.

● ● ●

GOOD OLD ROCK AND ROLL:
TEEN CULTURE IN THE EISENHOWER ERA

● ● ●

For the majority of its listeners, rock and roll was born more than a lifetime ago. The pop archaeologists point to 1954 as the year during which rock got off the ground and, in particular, make much of a recording called "Sh-Boom" by the Chords, a black group. "Sh-Boom" was a rhythm-and-blues hit which became so popular that it reached the top ten of the pop charts—the first rhythm-and-blues record to become a national pop hit. The rhythm-and-blues field in the nineteen fifties dealt with what had been known as race records—recordings by black artists for black listeners. It must be noted that back then it was felt that white young-sters should not listen to the same music as black young-sters because "Negro music" would inexorably lead to sexual promiscuity, idleness, miscegenation, crime, in-discriminate jiving, and other harbingers of the col-lapse of Western Civilization. When it became appar-ent that "Sh-Boom" was going to be a national hit, the song was "covered" (music-business argot meaning re-corded by someone other than the original performer) by a white group called the Crew Cuts, whose record-ing followed the original into the top ten. "Sh-Boom" was also covered by a number of other performers and even reached the British top ten later in the year. There were similar goings-on in 1955 when a number of other rhythm-and-blues hits, such as "Earth Angel" and "Goodnight, Irene, Goodnight," were covered by white pop singers.

"Sh-Boom" now sounds rather ridiculous, but it had a certain frantic authenticity that wasn't to be found in the pop hits of the day. Most important, "Sh-Boom"'s success made the music business aware of the commercial potential of rough rhythm-and-blues-type material, with its considerable appeal to a young, mass, white audience which was slowly starving on a diet of party-dressed chanteuses and superannuated big bands.

Nineteen fifty-four and 1955 also witnessed the emergence of Bill Haley and his band, the Comets, as the first rock-and-roll stars with the success of their recordings "Shake, Rattle and Roll," a cover of a Joe Turner number, and "Rock Around the Clock." Haley, a pudgy late-twenty-year-old former disk jockey and country-and-western musician, was a most unlikely candidate for popular adulation, with his fat face, greasy kiss curls, and garish plaid dinner jacket, but the novelty and appeal of his music was such that, even today, as he nears fifty, he and the Comets work steadily. Haley was heavily influenced by both rhythm-and-blues and country-and-western music, and ever since then both R&B and C&W, with their tight, guitar-oriented orchestration, have been constant sources of musical inspiration to rock performers.

But perhaps the major pop cultural event of those early years was the release of *Blackboard Jungle,* a film about a decaying urban high school within whose dingy walls idealistic young teachers struggle with callous old teachers to show compassion for their students; black students beat up on white students; white students beat up on black students; oversexed students molest innocent young women librarians; and both black and white students beat up both callous old and sensitive young teachers. *Blackboard Jungle* refined, distilled, and stylized the teen-ager as a j.d. (juvenile delinquent)—tough-talking, violent, black-leather-jacketed, white-tee-shirted, greasy haired, cruel yet sensitive, misunderstood. In a key scene, a sympathetic but quite pathetic young teacher tries to win his students' friendship by bringing his collection of rare 78-r.p.m. jazz records into class. Within minutes the records are lying on the floor, shattered, broken to bits by the students. "Sorry, teach," one of them mumbles. These hooligans don't want to know about 78s, daddyo, they've got rock and roll. And of course the film's theme song was "Rock Around the Clock," which made Bill Haley a transatlantic star and caused numerous outbreaks of riotous enthusiasm wherever the film was shown. Both the content of *Blackboard Jungle* and its reception seemed to say that these kids were dangerous.

Blackboard Jungle, Rebel Without a Cause, The

Wild One, and similar films of the time all helped to shape the public conception of the teen-ager. While people have always aged from twelve to twenty via years thirteen through nineteen, the teen-ager was invented by post-World War II America, a society affluent enough to postpone adulthood for many of its children. The teen-ager, in all his hideous guises, was a product of the prolonged adolescence spawned by the material abundance of modern America, and rock and roll was his music. Rock and roll became an inextricable part of the incipient teen-age folk culture.

But just what is rock and roll? Essentially, it's a mix of rhythm-and-blues and country-and-western music which developed in the mid-fifties. From its beginnings, rock and roll has been characterized by a preoccupation with the beat and an almost antiliterate lyric style which at first developed organically from teen-age slang (Crazy man, crazy) and black idiom and later became somewhat contrived. Rock and roll at its best has always been raw, sexy, a bit incoherent, and never afraid of being inelegant or just plain stupid.

Sex has always been an important part of rock music. Both in its lyric content and its style of presentation rock is the most overtly sexual form of pop music. While earlier songwriters like Cole Porter were sexy in a suave and stylish manner—coy, one might say—rock lyricists and performers have always gone in for, or at least aspired to, the "I-crave-your-body-and-I'm-going-to-have-it" cum "Sleep-with-me-or-I'll-bash-your-head-in" school of sexual etiquette. That this sexuality was derived principally from the tough rhythm-and-blues genre—witness Hank Ballard and the Midnighters' 1954 tunes, "Sexy Ways" and "Work with Me, Annie" —is undeniable, and it is equally undeniable that the sexual ethic of rock and roll was particularly appealing to the mid-fifties teen-age audience.

It would be misleading, however, to suggest that all rock songs treated sex in a direct and brutal way. Indeed, many songs of the fifties and early sixties treated sex indirectly, palliated with all the paraphernalia of mass-marketed commercial romance—angels, chapels, flowers, paradise, and even forever, which is a hell of a long time. But it is true that rock and roll deals with sex more frequently and more directly than any other popular art, and that lust, though certainly not the most interesting emotion, is unquestionably one of the strongest. Much of the speed and fervor with which rock and roll was adopted by millions of kids as their music must have been due to the outlet it offered a sexually frustrated and repressed audience.

Rock and roll also provided a measure of relief for all the social frustrations of the teen-age audience, and was a sort of metaphysical arena in which the impotent mass could do battle against their oppressors—parents, school authorities, bureaucrats, and others. This is not to suggest that rock and roll was the "Marseillaise" of a horde of flaming revolutionaries out to challenge and change the fundamental precepts of society. Rather, it was the mass grumble of those who felt that they deserved a bigger piece of the action. No mass art can exist without a willing audience, and it was the good fortune of the early rock-and-roll performers and entrepreneurs to be involved in the creation of a new musical style that appealed so strongly to a segment of the population that was to be in the economic and demographic ascendent for a long time.

Whether "Sh-Boom" or "Your Cash Aint Nothin' but Trash" was the first rock-and-roll recording is a chronological-musicological quibble which only obscures the music's early growth. What is important is that between 1954 and 1956 the music—a hybrid of black, country, and folk—and the audience—the American teen-ager—came together. And rock and roll has been with us ever since.

• • •

THE GOLDEN AGE OF ROCK AND ROLL?

• • •

Although much, indeed almost everything, has changed in the last two decades, rock and roll retains its congenital features: a derivative eclecticism drawing heavily upon black and country sources, a Neanderthalish sexuality, and a general though often tacit feeling of being a bit pissed-off at the world.

Many people consider the early years of rock and roll to be the genre's classic period. Such views, while understandable, are absolute nonsense. Many good songs were written and performed in those early years, and early rock and roll did have a laudable directness and vigor of presentation, but to look at the first years of rock and roll as an age of grace from which we have since fallen is only to indulge a specious and weak-minded aesthetic that views the past as a theater in which we can act out our inabilities to understand the present.

There are two other important qualities of rock and roll which date from its genitive period: its creative independence and its self-consciousness. By "creative independence" I do not mean any resistance to external inspiration, but a tendency from almost the very start for rock-and-roll performers to write their own material. Traditionally, this independence belongs more to the folk and blues genres than to pop music. Although at all times much rock music has been written

21

by nonperforming songwriters—for example, Leiber and Stoller, who wrote many great songs, including "Poison Ivy" and "Jailhouse Rock"—it has always been the songwriting performers who are most highly esteemed. Performers who consistently depend on others for their material often have short-lived careers. Perhaps this accounts for a major part of rock and roll's authenticity.

The music's self-consciousness may derive from its early status as "outsider's" music, nasty and unmelodic, not at all what Mother and Dad want Junior and Sis to listen to. In addition, rock and roll has long publicized itself as an art form, Chuck Berry's 1957 hit "Rock and Roll Music" being a particularly good example. Rock and roll songwriters, sensing at first the uncertain status of their music and then its cultural power, have always written rock-and-roll songs about rock and roll. This self-consciousness indicates an awareness of rock and roll not just as a musical style but also as the cultural focus of a generation.

The most significant figures of rock and roll's formative years—1954–1960—were two very different men: Elvis Presley and Chuck Berry. Presley was, for all his down-homey Southern piety and yesma'aming, a real glamor boy: a sexy, sulking, tough, macho hayseed. A performer of extraordinary style and personal projection, Elvis inspired unprecedented hysteria among his fans, sold records more quickly than anyone in music history, and gave rock and roll an image in the very best Hollywood star tradition—gold lamé suits, fleets of Cadillacs, and all that. Even though he was just a good ole boy, he gave rock and roll a much-needed infusion of glamor and glitter that someone like Bill Haley just couldn't provide.

Chuck Berry, though possessing great charm and

magnetism, was hardly in the film-star mold. A black, Midwestern, singer-guitarist-songwriter, Berry was the most musicianly of the early rock stars and possibly the most influential performer of the last twenty years. With his simple but tough guitar style and his wryly trenchant comments on the problems and paradoxes of modern life, Berry was the first performer to demonstrate that rock and roll could be artistically and philosophically worthwhile as well as good to dance to. Berry was the first to put a measure of quality into rock music and all current rock-and-roll performers and listeners must be inestimably in his debt.

The list of major rock-and-roll figures of the fifties is a long one and must include such performers as Buddy Holly, Jerry Lee Lewis, Eddie Cochrane, and the Everly Brothers. But in spite of the amount of creative and performing talent, it was apparent that by the end of the fifties rock and roll was beginning to run out of steam, as it were, and was becoming increasingly monotonous, formulaic, and uninventive. It seemed, in fact, to be going through a climacteric period after which it would just merge into the mainstream of popular music.

A number of reasons for this stagnation may be adduced, though no one of them is definitive. Rock and roll began to lack drive and direction as the major talents faded. Buddy Holly was killed in an airplane crash. Eddie Cochrane died in a fatal automobile accident while touring Britain. Elvis Presley was drafted into the army in 1958 and came out two years later with much of his musical vigor diminished. Chuck Berry's career was clouded by a morals charge involving an underage girl.

More and more rock material was being written by nonperforming songwriters and presented to the public by a variety of commercially palatable though singularly undistinguished performers. As the tremendous monetary potential of rock and roll was realized, the production and presentation of the music took on many of the features of any industrial process. The music became less frantic, less crazy, smoother, more romantic—altogether more acceptable. By 1960 rock and roll was on the skids as clean-cut and fresh-faced greaseballs like Bobby Rydell and Fabian were thrust in front of the public as the new rock stars. As the decade ended, rock and roll appeared to be firmly under the control of adults and businessmen, and the great congressional hearings of 1959–60, which investigated corruption in the music business, were symptomatic of rock's alienation from its audience. Rock and roll was becoming mere entertainment and abandoning its social and artistic role as an interpreter of the world for teen-age Americans.

• • •

TECHNOCULTING SPUTNIK AND COLD WAR ACTION

• • •

The United States reached 1960 with its national psyche a bit scarred because things just hadn't worked out as they were supposed to. It was most upsetting, because the United States, for whatever mistakes it has made, has always been distinguished by a sense of moral urgency—a need to set the world right—and until 1950 all had gone more or less according to plan. The Spaniards had enslaved the lovable and neighborly Cubans, so we sent them packing back to Barcelona and made Cuba free; the Kaiser raped Belgium and told his U-boats to do nasty things to ocean liners loaded with innocent women and children, so we sent Pershing and his crusaders overseas to bash Wilhelm in the pickelhaub; Hitler wanted to rule the world, so we tromped him; and as for those dastardly Japs, they just had to be nuked, and let that be a lesson that no one messes with Uncle Sam. It was all very uplifting, rewarding, and quite satisfying, but things began to go quite wrong when the leaders of the Free World decided that the Commies had gone just too far, and Korea was the result.

Korea was just not the sort of war to which America was accustomed—it was grimy, obscure, uninspired, and, to make things much worse, it wasn't even a victory, just a draw. The Korean War was perhaps the first sign that the post-World War II world was going to be a pretty rough place to live in as American ideology became less and less an accurate reflection of the realities of life. The growing strength and truculence of the Communist nations were especially troublesome, as it had always been a tenet of the American faith that right makes might and no nation that sent its dissidents out into the boondocks to labor in salt mines could be right.

The major jolt to the already tottering American sense of self-confidence was the USSR's launching of the first artificial earth satellite in 1957. The entire tradition of Yankee ingenuity and American technical know-how was shattered in an instant, and, good God, if Russky could pull off something as clever as Sputnik, he might even be able to H-bomb us into oblivion before you could say Strategic Air Command. The era's forte was the piling of anxiety upon anxiety.

The American response was the launching of the Explorer satellite in the following year and a massive shift toward an educational policy that favored scientific and technical programs of instruction. It became quite glamorous for Joe Student to stroll across the campus of Anyville College with a cheerleader in one hand and a slide rule in the other. Space fever of a sort struck the United States as superpower politics was played out in the firmament, and Detroit did its bit to help by producing the most garishly designed automobiles yet seen—cars with chrome rockets shooting out of front grille and rear bumper alike and enormous rakish rocket fins rising out of back fenders. So after a bit of a setback the U.S. was once again holding its own, but it was getting to be hard work.

Nineteen sixty was quite appropriately a Significant Year as Americans faced the new decade—dubbing it the "Soaring Sixties" in contrast to the bleak but "Fabulous Fifities"—with the faith and confidence that with some work and sufficient quantities of rectitude and apple pie, our Way of Life would endure and triumph. Benign, grandfatherly, ineffectual General Eisenhower went back to the farm, and witty, young, glamorous, charming, aristocratic John Kennedy arrived at the White House.

JFK seemed to be the herald of a new order of things—a President who laughed, was clever, and didn't look like someone's uncle. With JFK at the helm, how could we lose?

The first sugar in the gas tank of the new decade was tossed by Fidel Castro, a radical young lawyer—the decade was to be a great one for radical young lawyers—who rather upset the State Department by seizing power in Cuba and then becoming the Western Hemisphere's first Communist head of state and leading revolutionary. The U.S. government's 1961 attempt to oust Fidel by supporting a dime-store invasion by anti-Communist Cuban refugees landed at the Bay of Pigs was both a failure and an embarrassment. But surely the most dangerous and terrifying event of those years was the Soviet construction of missile installations in Cuba. The ensuing missile crisis of 1962, during which the U.S. successfully forced the USSR to remove its missiles from Cuba, was a chilling exemplar of brinksmanship. It seemed then as if nuclear war was imminent and that those few of us who survived the Big One would spend the rest of our days eating canned beef in fallout shelters telling legends about the Sun.

For a season the fur-coated dowagers shivered from more than the air conditioning in the lobbies of Miami Beach hotels as those filthy upstart, troublesome Cubans played the dagger in the softest part of the Free World's underbelly. But even as Fidel and his boys were scaring the shit out of the nation there was something admirable and even inspiring about them. In a way they set the style for the home-grown activists of the coming decade—bearded, unkempt, scruffily dressed in dingy military fatigues—a stunning example of the small, dedicated revolutionary band that sets the world off balance. At a time when youthful protesters wore chino pants and button-down shirts and took tea with Presidential advisors while discussing the Nuclear Test Ban Treaty, the romantic appeal of revolution, even as carried out by nasty, Russky-loving revolutionaries, must have been strong, though it was to remain unarticulated for some years.

The unfortunate Cuban affair was something of a triumph for Kennedy. For a terrifying moment the world had one foot in the nuclear grave, and it seemed that it was only the intelligence and daring of the President and his men that saw us through. To the popular mind it was the sort of thing that only a cool, young President was capable of pulling off.

More than at any time in its recent history, the

United States was captivated by one man. Kennedy the President was not really such a great statesman or politician, but Kennedy as a cultural leader and symbol was a figure of such charm that nothing seemed wrong, or at least not able to be set right, so long as the force of his personality pervaded the nation and the world. It was unbearably cruel, as only history can be, when a maniac put a bullet through JFK's head on that sunny November day in Dallas in 1963. No one can erase the special horror of that Friday, and for the young, to whom Kennedy was such a special person, it was Fate's message that nothing is safe from destruction.

Nineteen sixty-three must be remembered as a year of loss, bitterness, and despair in which a feeling began to grow that death was the reward for goodness. The world seemed to be a less decent place and the feeling that we had been betrayed by the powers above was to linger on for many years after.

In an odd way JFK and Castro were linked not just as adversaries in a diplomatic incident but as exemplars of two different approaches to the same time in history: Kennedy as the decent, humanistic, conventional statesman who was senselessly murdered, and Fidel as the ruthless rebel who seized and subjugated Fortune, if only for a time. The lesson learned by the young in those few years when the careers of the two men met was not to be lost.

THE COMING OF
THE NEW ROCK
1964-1966

● ● ●

THE BEATLES AND
THE BRITISH INVASION

● ● ●

The seventh decade of the century stalled shortly after takeoff, and by early 1964 the signs of moral and cultural bathos were unmistakable. The American pop music scene was especially dreary as the crude intensity of early rock and roll was replaced by the more sophisticated and socially wholesome musical garbage which was being peddled by the pop merchants of the time. A glance at some of the hits of 1963 is interesting: "Surfer Bird" by the Rivingtons, "Two Faces Have I" by Lew Christie, "It's My Party" by Leslie Gore—nothing too inspiring or vigorous there. Black artists continued to turn out listenable and vital music, like Martha and the Vandellas' "Heat Wave" and Rufus

Thomas's "Walking the Dog," but things were pretty bleak and the growing new musical trends, surfing music and folk (which we shall talk about later), hardly spoke to the mass in quite the same way that early rock had.

The arrival of the Beatles on the American music scene was one of those events of shattering and irreversible significance which, while not so important to the course of history as the invention of the stirrup or the French Revolution, was analogous in its impact on a part of society—afterward things were never the same. The enthusiasm—no, fanaticism—with which the Beatles were received by the music-buying public was not directly a reaction to the quality of life and music being dealt out in the grim days of late 1963, but there is no doubt that the unsatisfactory temper of life and entertainment at the time made the Beatles' arrival all the more stunning. The Beatles were truly the much-needed cultural antidote to the vague malaise that kids were feeling.

The details of the Beatles' lives and careers are well covered elsewhere and only of concern to fans. The big question isn't Does Paul like chocolate pudding? or What size shoes does Ringo wear? but How did four blokes from Liverpool change the world's ideas about pop music as the Beatles did? Before the Beatles the rock and roller was either an unkempt outlaw who wore a black-leather jacket, played guitar, made sexually suggestive body movements, and sang about how hard it was to be young and in love, or else he was a clean-cut, cardigan-sweatered, slightly greasy but cute boy-next-door type who sang about how hard it was to be young and in love. After the Beatles the rock performer began to be seen not just as an entertainer but as a social visionary, a cultural trend-setter, a questing, fashionable, archetypal citizen of a new society—Beau Brummell, William Blake, and Thomas Jefferson rolled into one and put on stage with an electric guitar. The Beatles expanded the conception and scope of operations of pop music and made rock and roll the centerpiece of an entire youthful culture. After the Beatles people began to look toward rock and roll not only for their musical entertainment but also for their politics and life-style.

The British pop scene of the late fifties and early sixties was a particularly dismal nursery for talents of the Beatles' magnitude, dominated as it was by good-looking but, sadly, not very talented rock singers in the American mold. The only true British pop style to develop in those days was skiffle (e.g., "Rock Island Line" as performed by Lonnie Donegan), a popped-up variety of folk music, which was always more of a novelty than a musical style that could offer much scope for development. The British rock singers were always just too far removed from the sources of rock influence—rhythm and blues, and country and western—and they lacked the authenticity of the better American rock and rollers. Even the outstanding British performers like Cliff Richard, Billy Fury, and Tommy Steel really didn't have it, and while they were enormously popular in the U.K. they failed to make any impact on the American market. In all the early years of rock only three British performers—Lonnie Donegan, Laurie London, and a group called the Tornadoes, who were largely the creation of producer Joe Meek—were American chart successes. On the other hand, American performers consistently did well in Britain. It is important, though, that British performers, particularly Cliff Richard, appealed to a much wider age group than American rock performers. For example Cliff Richard's

1959 hit, "Living Doll," wasn't really rock and roll at all. This same type of appeal that went beyond the teen-age part of the population and the ability to perform non-rock material and still be a rock and roll performer was to figure in the Beatles' success.

Nothing in the Beatles' early lives marked them for greatness: they weren't Eton and Oxbridge boys who read Heidegger and one day decided to become missionaries of a new youth culture—they were just the children of working-class Liverpudlians, just kids who played a bit of skiffle, listened to records, and decided to get a rock group together. They had a long and hard slog playing in small and squalid rock clubs in Britain and Germany, and they became the Beatles. They had the good fortune to get a sensitive, neurotic, hard-working manager in the person of Brian Epstein; a recording contract with EMI; and an astute producer named George Martin.

The Beatles' commercial success was startling. After their first single, "Love Me Do," reached the number seventeen position in the British charts in 1962, they had a string of number one songs beginning with "Please, Please Me" in 1963 and continuing with "She Loves You," "I Want to Hold Your Hand," and just about everything else they released for a number of years. The Beatles' arrival in the United States in 1964 was heralded by tales of their commercial success in Britain and their frenzied reception by British youth. Their first American release, "I Want to Hold Your Your Hand," quickly became the best-selling record in the United States, and by April the five most popular singles were all Beatles' records.

But the Beatles were not just big record sellers. They inspired absolute hysteria in their fans—the screaming of audiences at their concerts was so loud that often the Beatles couldn't be heard by the audience. Audiences were involved to an almost frightening degree as young girls sobbed, fainted, and even wet their little seats. The audience were no longer mere receivers of entertainment; they were part of the show, which was rather closer in feeling to the Nuremburg Rally than to a traditional concert. This new, intense relationship between performer and audience raised more than a few totalitarian ghosts, and the possibility of mass control through pop music was thought about as a possible future danger. This theme was treated most interestingly by Peter Watkins in his 1967 film, *Privilege.* 1925097

The Beatles were a phenomenon not just because of the magnitude of their commercial success (it was estimated that over half the single records sold in the United States in the spring of 1964 were Beatles records) or because of the fervor of their fans (singers like Frank Sinatra and Johnny Ray had had it before) but because of the qualitative nature of their success. People realized intuitively that the Beatles were not just a passing craze; they had staying power. A glance at the covers of the first Beatles albums shows quite literally the new image that the boys demanded. At the time album covers were most often either pedestrianly cute or sexless male pin-up glossy color photographs of healthily glowing artists. While the Beatles' first album cover was nothing special, their second cover featured a stark high-fashion photograph by Robert Freeman— a grainy black-and-white close shot of the group in black jerseys against a black backdrop. The message was that these boys belong in *Vogue,* not just *Hit Parader.*

The Beatles finally made rock and roll socially acceptable. Their evolving chic visual image coupled with their musical eclecticism—one of their most popular early tunes was that paragon of schlock, "Til There Was You"—secured for them a wide audience. The twist craze of 1961 was actually the first time that rock and roll became *à la mode;* the Duke of Bedford, Noel Coward, Lee Radziwill, and the usual bore of jet setters were all quite keen on that amusing little number, the twist. But the Beatles were the first rock group to capitalize on the aging-though-socially-elite's desire to be young and "with it."

The Beatles were able to do this because they were musically and culturally more palatable than their predecessors. They had a certain exotic appeal to Americans. While someone like Chubby Checker might be found pumping gas at the local service station, you just wouldn't find the Beatles doing such a thing. I mean, not four boys with accents like George Sanders. Moreover, they had a sense of melody and they enunciated clearly. They were the first rock group about whom middle-aged couples didn't say, "I can't understand a thing they're saying, dear. It all sounds like noise to me." They even sang in harmony: "But I thought that only the Mills Brothers sang in harmony, dear."

The Beatles sang, played, and composed with an easy vitality and vigor that even the first rock performers lacked. They sang constantly about love: enthusiastic, carefree, optimistic. The Beatles were bright and cheerful and fun. Their music and their attitude toward life were characterized by an insouciance that was perhaps a reaction to the grimness of life in an economically and socially declining city like Liverpool. The Beatles knew that Britain as a great power was on the skids and said So What, "All You Need Is Love"—a far cry indeed from Kipling and G.A. Henty. This was the quiddity of the Beatles' message: the subordination of all things to love and the enjoyment of what you have. The Beatles didn't pretend to be serious young men or model citizens or representatives of any special interest. They sang about and celebrated youth because they themselves were young, and through the force and appeal of their personalities helped to create an international youth cult. For a time, everybody wanted to be young, even kids. The Beatles ended the social alienation of kids trying to act like adults, but unfortunately they intensified the even more grotesque social alienation of adults trying to be kids.

As mentioned earlier, the stylistic range of the Beatles' music was remarkable; they performed standard old rock numbers, Broadway musical tripe, and their own compositions with equal ease. Although they began to play their own songs almost exclusively after their first two albums, they composed in an amazing variety of styles, ensuring themselves a larger and more heterogeneous audience than any other performers in pop music.

Adding to the appeal of the Beatles' musical variety were their own differences of personality. Paul McCartney was cherubic, sweet and almost unbearably cute; John Lennon was a moody and whimsical intellectual; George Harrison was a tough, stringy rock and roller; and Ringo Starr was the slightly pathetic, nebishy but completely lovable outsider.

As musical performers the Beatles were, with the exception of Paul McCartney's outstanding bass playing, undistinguished, and as vocalists it was once again only McCartney who had outstanding talent. But throughout their career the group played with that undefinable extramusical spirit that elevated all their performances far above the commonplace. It was the Beatles' extraordinary songwriting ability and the almost palpable force of their personalities that raised them to such heights, in the process changing them from rock and roll singers to cultural leaders of great influence and considerable staying power. Today, well over a decade after their initial success and six years after their breakup as a group, all four Beatles continue to have great popularity as individual recording artists.

A horde of British groups rose to prominence in the wake of the Beatles. Varying in quality from the very very good—the Rolling Stones, the Who, or the Animals—to the not so hot—Tommy Quickly or the Fourmost. Of course no two rock groups could be less alike than, say, the Beatles and the Rolling Stones, but all the British rock groups were characterized by a fresh and vigorous approach to rock and roll. As outstanding as the Beatles were, they were not sui generis but were part of a general scene which was particularly intense around Liverpool and spawned dozens of rock groups. Because the Beatles were better than any of the other groups, and because they were the first to be presented to a wider audience, they eased the way for the other British groups by creating a new climate of opinion in the American music market that made British groups not only acceptable but eminently desirable. Some American bands, like the Beau Brummels, even found it necessary to copy the British style quite literally. While it is true that there has always been a high degree of Anglo-American cultural exchange and fluidity—witness T.S. Eliot, Henry James, Whistler and others—the advent of the Beatles and the other British groups who followed them marked the first time since Yorktown that the mass of young Americans began to look toward Britain as a source of cultural supply and inspiration.

● ● ●

POP STYLE AND THE
FASHION RENASCENCE

● ● ●

Why did the focus of pop-music culture shift so swiftly and dramatically from the United States to Britain? As with any reasonably interesting question there are a number of possible answers. Pop culture, as opposed to folk culture, is the product of an affluent mass-market society, and as mass affluence came later to Britain than to the United States, British pop culture in the postwar years tended to be modeled after and influenced by American films, music and so on. As modern pop culture wasn't indigenous to Britain, it may have been more studiously and consciously thought about by British creative artists and intellects: surely the first awareness of the aesthetic significance of the commonplace objects and appliances of modern mass affluence was expressed in Britain by people like Richard Hamilton and the school of pop artists that followed him.

In the early sixties Britain was also going through a temporary period of prosperity, which seemed particularly intense after the bleak austerity of the immediate postwar years. Under the "You never had it so good" premiership of Harold Macmillan the British public was frantically trying to make up for the forgone consumption of the past years. Coupled with this was the growing realization, especially after Suez, that Britain was no longer to be burdened with the responsibilities of world power, and so the imperial mantle could be exchanged for clothing of a more comfortable and altogether more frivolous nature.

Although Britain was becoming a much less important country on the world scene, there was, I think, a mood of buoyant optimism and relief in the nation in the late fifties and early sixties. As America went through the torments of Reds at the doorstep, racial conflict, and the Kennedy assassination, the British were able for the first time to enjoy the benefits of the consumer society on a large scale. Thus the downswing in the American national mood was countered by a vigorous and expansive concern with the less important aspects of life by the British. Whereas the British had once exported law, locomotives, and capital, after 1964 they exported rock groups, trendy clothing, and various accouterments of popular youth culture. London once again became a world city and was, if only for a brief while, the home of all that was desirable in modern life —"Swinging London," as certified by *Time* magazine.

The pervasiveness of rock and roll in British popular culture was extraordinary. Rock and roll was fashionable; it was no longer just for kids or for one social class. The Beatles played for the Royal Family and at the same time Britain had its strongest Labour government in years. Much of the British popular aesthetic of the time was tasteless in the extreme, yet it was all very exciting and somehow quite appalling in the way it sacrificed everything to be *au courant*. The cheap and flashy clothing which people bought, wore, and discarded with alarming rapidity and the extremely out-of-context modernity of the General Post Office tower, which still jars the London skyline, are just two examples of what was going on in Britain at the time. Britain in the early to mid-sixties was once again the center of the English-speaking world's attention.

Although the importance of the Beatles and the Rolling Stones to the British cultural scene at the time can hardly be denied, the two groups must be seen not as a cause of the pop ferment of those years. Rather, they were the products of and the most brilliant advertisement for the variety and energy of a cultural complex that produced and was produced by people like Mary Quant, David Hockney, John Stephen, Brian Epstein, Screaming Lord Sutch, Vidal Sassoon, Jean Shrimpton, and all the other members of the motley army of artists, fashion designers, rock musicians, entrepreneurs and trendy people who made swinging London swing. The London-centered pop culture of the time was more concerned with trendiness than with traditional ideas of taste and artistic philosophy. In such a milieu content becomes necessarily subordinate to presentation if for no other reason than that the pressure to be more up to date than everyone else forces one to devote all one's energies to thinking of newer and commercially better means of presentation. This is essentially what both fashion and pop music are about. In fashion the contents—the body—remain the same; only the package—clothing—changes. In Beatles-era Britain, fashion and pop music were more closely allied than ever before.

The early sixties were years of major change in the world of fashion. The entrepreneurial and commercial talent of British designers and rag traders absorbed, modified, and marketed the startling stylistic innovations of high-fashion designers like Courrèges and, later, Cardin.

The major fashion developments of the time were the redefinition of women's clothing, the reintroduction of stylistic change and flash into men's clothes, and the lengthening of men's hair. Sparked by the stark designs of André Courrèges and the sales and design sense of Mary Quant, women's clothing became increasingly stark, stylized, abstract, and revealing. The look of the fifties, in which women's upper halves were practically rocketed out of volcanic masses of chiffon which hid them from the waist down, was replaced by the simpler, harsher lines of ever shorter dresses which placed more stress on legs than ever before. The new fashion required a new female type to wear it and so necessitated the invention of the dolly bird: a slim and starkly attractive young thing (whose archetype was the model Jean Shrimpton) with large, limpid, blue eyes, straight blond hair, and legs up to here. Dolly birds were lissome, coltish, and icily impassive. They wore Yardley cosmetics, spent most of the day shopping, and most of the evening hopping out of white Jaguar convertibles driven by aristocratic young men who took them dancing at fashionable clubs and discotheques. The dolly birds were clothes hangers for the new fashions and indispensable accessories for the new pop way of life.

The changes in men's fashion, while perhaps less innovative visually, were quite shocking, as color and style once again became fashion factors for men. The disappearance of color and style from men's fashion in the nineteenth century is an interesting phenomenon in the history of taste. Industrialization, which produced a rising standard of mass clothing, had moderated the formerly extreme class differences in fashion while also producing a social ethic that favored sobriety and a certain functional decorum. Except under the most extreme conditions of labor, symbolic considerations have usually been more important than functional considerations in the design of costume. Even after the Greek Revival has been taken into account, there was actually very little nineteenth-century reaction against the stylistic excesses of the previous century, as a glance at Victorian or Second Empire furniture and architecture will bear witness to. But while the ecclesiastical and military garb of the nineteenth century continued to be as resplendent as ever, new attitudes about the respectability of economic activity among the upper classes, who were the style leaders, dictated that men's wear should reflect the dignity and seriousness of business enterprise, and this remained the governing concept of men's clothing throughout the first half of this century. Rumblings of high style in our times began with the "Continental Look" of Italian tailoring in the fifties, but fashion as a series of changing clothing styles was largely confined to groups who weren't in the social mainstream—teen-agers, laborers out for a night on the town, and college students with their constant fads in both clothing and behavior. And, of course, rock performers and other entertainers. But it wasn't until the advent of the British pop groups that rock musicians became accepted as style leaders.

The British rock groups tended to pick up much of their fashion from the earlier "Mod" movement. The Mods were an extraordinary bunch of mostly London street kids who devoted all their creative energies to designing and wearing clothes. This implied that clothing was more than just packaging—it could be an aesthetic and social end in itself. Fashion then began to travel hand in hand with pop music as yet another way of bringing attention to the musical product. Who could possibly ignore a band dressed in the foppish finery of the Kinks or the aggressive modness of the Who? The rock groups repopularized old materials like velvet, suede, and leather and made "dressing up" an integral part of their style. There's nothing very visually pleasing about the British pop clothes of the time—the Beatles with their collarless jackets and high-heeled pointed-toe cabretta leather boots, for example—but the attitiude of having fun with clothing, of visualizing one's outfit as a work of art and of using clothing to express the freneticism of the pop society was laudable and healthy.

• • •

 HAIR AND HISTORY

• • •

The history of male hairstyles is similar to that of clothing, that is, the long and elaborate Baroque and rococo hairstyles were superseded by the shorter and more severe looking creations of the nineteenth and twentieth centuries. Yet throughout the period of change from long to short hair the almost deliberate anachronism of long hair was identified with romanticism (not Romanticism) and creativity, as a look at some of the most relentlessly individual characters of the nineteenth century—men as different as Rossetti, George Armstrong Custer, and Longfellow—will attest. This should hardly be construed as saying that the progressive and creative members of society have always had long hair, but by 1960 anyone with long hair was thought to be quite bohemian—either a symphony conductor, a mystical poet, or some kind of fruitcake. The United States was a particularly short-haired nation as the sixties rolled in, home of the flat top, the crew cut, and other equally repulsive coifs. Although some of the older rockers had longer than average hair, such rocker hair-dos were usually piled up or brushed back and held in place with copious quantites of grease rather than allowed to hang down and look long.

When they first appeared before American audiences, the Beatles and the other British bands excited as much comment about their hairstyles as about their music. To the public, such extremely long hair—though it now looks quite short to us—could only be a sign of homosexuality, communism, or irreversible brain damage. Disregarding the warnings of their elders and wisers, American teen-agers began growing their hair longer in emulation of the new rock idols, and the ineluctable creep from "just leave it long over the ears" to "just leave it long over the shoulders" had begun. Long-haired kids were discriminated against, called fags and Reds, beaten up and made the object of much scorn, yet the new long hairstyles persisted and gradually were adopted by aging executives and others not generally regarded as being in the vanguard of pop culture.

For a few years long hair was a sign of a certain degree of social and sexual liberation on the part of the wearer—an indication of a willingness to flout the canon of "neat + modest = masculine." Long hair was often quite repulsive-looking but it was initially a small way of saying "up-yours" to society and in that way a small victory for the individual personality. Under the conditions of the affluent mass society—which provides a decent standard of material comfort, but often at the price of too much conformity and blandness—it is crucial that people should be allowed to express their individuality if only in the negative way of saying, "I won't wear my hair as everyone else does." Fads, fashions, and pop music are the safety valves of modern society, providing a means of individual expression while not threatening the conformist consensus which is essential to our way of life. Unfortunately, such nonconformism creates its own tyranny; those with the wrong length hair or the wrong style of Beatle boots may be sneered at. But life isn't all sweetness and light, and such intolerance is an inevitable result of the need for social solidarity among those groups who are in revolt against prevailing standards of taste.

Long hair signified rock and roll more than anything. The Beatles wear their hair long, I like the Beatles, I wear my hair long. Simple enough, and the tenacity with which young people adopted long hair and withstood the many inconveniences they were subjected to because of it indicates just how seriously rock fashion and style could be taken. Just as merely listening to rock and roll a decade earlier was a sign of revolt, so the wearing of long hair and the new pop clothing styles was a rebellion against established standards of fashion and a way of expressing one's aesthetic allegiance.

The pop scene had something of a one-world movement about it as audiences adopted the same visual styles wherever British rock became popular. While it is naïve to think that the adoption of fads on an international basis will bring us into a new era of international harmony and understanding, the rapid spread of rock fashion from Britain to the U.S. and other countries did create a certain aesthetic community of interest among young people. Most important, the linking of rock and roll with the new fashions made life nicer and more interesting by once again adding fun and expressiveness to dressing, which had previously been regarded far too often as just another drab and tiresome necessity.

● ● ●

DECADANCING IN THE NIGHT
—THE ROLLING STONES

● ● ●

The Rolling Stones were the flip side of Britain's pop-music consciousness in the mid-sixties. The Beatles were smooth, melodic, a bit sophisticated, clean, and

cheery, while the Rolling Stones were scruffy, unkempt, mean, and quite distasteful by contemporary
standards. Socially, the Stones were working- and middle-class boys from Greater London. Musically, they
began their careers as members of the small circle of
British blues musicians who derived their music from
some of the sources of early rock and roll—black American blues singers like Muddy Waters (from one of
whose songs the Stones took their name) and Howling
Wolf. That American blues music was ignored by most
young musicians in the United States but seized upon
with great fervor in Britain is curious. Perhaps it was
because British rock musicians were geographically
one step removed, and a very long step at that, from the
sources of rock and roll that the more dedicated among
them found it necessary to go more deeply into the
roots of rock and to pass from rhythm and blues back
into the real blues.

As a result of this musical digging, a number of
young British musicians sat in a number of cellars playing blues guitar and singing, "Ah's gwan to de station,
ah's gwan to catch a train." Yet out of the pretention
and bad musicianship which inevitably resulted from
such plagiarism, a sizable group of talented and musically sensible British musicians emerged. Chief among
them, and as it turned out the *éminence grise* of a whole
school of rock musicianship, was Alexis Korner, a quite
bizarre, gravel-voiced singer and guitarist under whose
tutelage many of Britain's best rock-and-roll musicians
were schooled. In the early sixties the then inchoate
Rolling Stones were among Korner's chief disciples,
and the Stones' first proper performances were greatly
helped by Korner's guidance and encouragement.

Just as the Beatles were part of a complex of Mersy-
side beat groups, so the Rolling Stones were the pro-

ducts of a large school of British blues bands which also included John Mayall, the Animals, the Yardbirds, the Graham Bond Organization and others. In contrast to the Beatles and the beat groups like the Searchers or Gerry and the Pacemakers, the Rolling Stones and the blues-influenced bands were rather more removed from the pop-music mainstream, and were musicianly in an almost scholastic sense as they studied and tried to get down the style of black American bluesmen. At the beginning they were not very good, and in most comparisons with original American blues recordings the performances of the British players will suffer even more than the listener. But the philosophy and structural simplicity of the blues provided fertile ground in which the talent of a number of British musicians could flourish.

I don't wish to make too rigid or artificial a distinction between the two major schools of British rock performers of the early sixties: both the Beatles and the Rolling Stones performed songs by Chuck Berry; the Stones' first hit, "I Wanna Be Your Man," was written for them by the Beatles; and there was much crossing of musical boundaries by all. But the Stones and the blues-inspired bands were in general a meaner and moodier lot because of their musical and occasionally social identification with American blacks. So rock again received a strong injection of social protest, though this time the protest changed from being an explicit message to being implicit in the overall style of the performers themselves.

That the Stones were the first pop group who didn't dress in a uniform fashion and who looked like a bunch of punks hauled off the nearest street corner was an essential part of their musical performance. Just as the Beatles with their tremendous stylistic range liberated rock and roll creatively, the Stones with their tough rebellious manner were the great social liberators of rock. The Stones were something special for every kid who wanted to wear blue jeans to high school and who didn't want to comb his hair. A few years later, the impact of their incredible commercial success made raunchy scruffiness a fashionable look, permitting high-society types like Jackie Onassis to run around in blue jeans and tee shirts. From quite early on in their careers, at least from their second album with its superbly trendy David Bailey–photographed cover, the Stones were destined to be the rock-and-roll totems of fashionable society.

Throughout their career, which is remarkable for both its longevity and the consistently high quality of their musical output, the Stones have thrived and profited from a social order which their art has consistently damned. But the Stones can't be accused of hypocrisy; they're pop entertainers who tell people what they want to hear and often do it better and more thought-provokingly than anyone else.

But the Rolling Stones' chief asset has always been the enormous collective power of their personalities. More than the Beatles, whose personal appeal derived in a large part from their talent as songmakers, the people would gladly pay to see the Rolling Stones just stand around and look like pop stars. Of course, the leading Stone in this respect is Mick Jagger, who may be the greatest performer in the history of pop music. Jagger projects himself with such force that it is difficult to describe him without resorting to the words usually attached to him: sexy, arrogant, stylish, androgynous, shrewd, intelligent, and whatever others come into one's mind. Whether Jagger really is sexy, arrogant, stylish, androgynous, shrewd, intelligent and whatever is quite irrelevant, for to the fans the reality of Jagger is Jagger on stage, on record, and in the press, where he regularly and unfailingly fulfills everyone's fantasies about him.

Alongside Jagger were the Stones' two guitarists: Keith Richard—snarling, ratty-looking, and an avatar of pop stardom—and Brian Jones—blond, wasted, girlishly beautiful and almost Jagger's equal. (Jones was forced to quit the band in 1969 following protracted musical and personal conflict with Jagger and Richard and died accidentally soon after leaving.) With the support of their stolid rhythm section of Bill Wyman and Charlie Watts, the three leading Stones oozed stardom from every fiber.

Stardom is and always has been independent of talent or genius. Star quality is what makes one person more compelling than another person of equal or even greater ability. The concept of stardom was born of the mass market, in which it is necessary to convince a body of undiscriminating consumers that one person rather than another should be the object of their artistic patronage. But star quality truly exists, and although the intensity of anyone's personality can be grossly exaggerated by the proper manipulation of the media, star quality can't be manufactured. Wellington had it but Blucher didn't; U.S. Grant had it but McClellan didn't. The Rolling Stones unquestionably have star quality, and a large part of their success must be due to the image they project and their way of life rather than to their musical ability.

The media potentates would have us believe that the public is meant to need them for diversion and amusement, as a link between art producer and art consumer and as an outlet for their fantasies. Stars are even an art form in themselves, in that their lives and images are a model of existence that's easier to understand than their art.

The Stones had it all. They were glamorous in an unwholesome and degenerate way; they did nasty and antisocial things like smoking dope; they were crude and sexy in a studied but quite authentic way; they were the sort of kids your parents wouldn't let you bring into the house. And they played with the same rude energy that had started the rock revolution. The Stones' music and their style is social criticism, an art of complaint and dissatisfaction with society which was well suited to the mood of 1964 and has somewhat sadly remained most appropriate for most of the past decade. The Stones have never been a "downer" group, though; they have always tried and often succeeded in giving their listeners a lift, and in that sense they may be more solidly in the tradition of popular entertainment than most other rock musicians. The Stones have never ignored their audience: they have always been hard working and concerned and responsible to their public. They may even be the best rock-and-roll band ever.

● ● ●
THE BRITISH ASCENDANCY
● ● ●

Although musical fashion evolved, the British pop scene in the mid-sixties is more accurately viewed as a confusing, often self-consciously frenetic hotbed of musical beasts and beauties than as an orderly and progressive era in the development of pop music. What is perhaps most remarkable about the time (1964–66)—surely more remarkable than the actual quality of the music that was produced—was the endless energy, vigor, and enthusiasm of all involved, musicians and audiences alike. There was a dedicated and passionate involvement in a cultural activity that was fun and fleeting, uncolored by any sense of profundity and pretention and lacking the turgid and inane pseudointellectualism and sanctimonious self-congratulation which was to be a feature of the later, more "mature" rock and roll.

The British pop scene was a carnival cum laboratory for social behavior in that the new pop idols extended the practice of dressing up and acting like a clown from the profession of actors and eccentrics to the social mode of the mass of young people. This democratization of buffoonery, as it were, was a product of the changing social, economic, and sartorial climate of Britain in the sixties; impelled and advertised by a horde of British rock groups, it proliferated internationally. The missionaries of this new secular faith of rock and roll, flash clothing, and youth were hardly a crusading band of militant pop-culture Jesuits. Yet in the aggregate they were a potent cultural force, their musical and personal differences moderated and dominated by their adherence to *le style pop-mod-anglais*— a philosophy of life-style rather than of life or music.

Bound together by their exuberance and fashionability, the British rock groups had greater strength as the promoters of a style of life and of a way of looking at life than as creative musical personalities. Nonetheless the musical variety and inventiveness of the times can't be easily discounted, and although no great musical breakthroughs may have been made, the swinging British scene at its zenith produced some quite exciting and moving pop music and schooled many of the musicians who continue to figure prominently in rock music.

While our view of the recent past must invariably

be refracted by the viscous emotionalism of nostalgia, one can make the attempt to listen dispassionately to the music produced by decade-old passions. After consigning quite a bit of that music to the aesthetic junk heap, one still finds an amazing amount of music which against its will has become relatively classic and is as entertaining and interesting as any pop music that has been produced in the interim.

It should be made clear that the Beatles and the Rolling Stones, for all their cosmic-musical-fashion-political-social significance, were not giants in a crowd of dwarfs. Listening back to records by some of the musical pygmies like Lulu, Tommy Quickly, Herman's Hermits, the Gear, Wayne Fontana, Dave Dee Dozy Beeky Mick and Tich, and all the other performers like them may still be quite fun, but more for nostalgic than musical reasons, since most of them were pretty rotten by almost any standards. But rock-and-roll music is so tangled into a whole subculture that *in vitro* analysis is a near impossibility. There were standout performers, though—those whose aesthetic integrity (relative to the pop genre), force of personality, and directness distinguished them from the others in the pack. Some, like the Who, are still creating; others, like the Spencer Davis Group, passed to the discount record shop in the sky long ago.

The Who in particular deserve special consideration, not only because they remain one of the premier rock groups in the world, but because from the start they established themselves as original talents and unflagging propagandists, visually and lyrically, of pop culture. The Who—Pete Townshend, Roger Daltrey, John Entwhistle, and Keith Moon—began life as a rhythm-and-blues group called the High Numbers, but after finding little success, changed their name, dressed as outrageously mod as possible—sports jackets made out of union jacks and the like—and began to record a string of Townshend-written songs which wittily and savagely (in both music and lyrics) dealt with generational hatred, masturbation, and other previously unarticulated subjects lurking in the back of teen-age minds yet ignored by previous rock songwriters. The Who's first big hit, "My Generation," was blunt ("Hope I die before I get old") and tough with its berserkly beaten drums and deafeningly loud bass guitar line, yet played and sung with the musical finesse and sophistication that have always distinguished the Who's music.

The Who were tougher and could be more distasteful than the Rolling Stones, even though their music and lyrics were rather more intellectual, because they knew how to use sonic brutality as a musical device. It was not a style of playing that they were locked into by stupidity or incompetence, as was the case with many other pop rock groups. Four gorillas equipped with electric guitars and amplifiers can make a hell of a racket; four musically intelligent and sophisticated rock musicians can make an even more unpleasant noise, but it will be sensible and purposeful.

The Who were talented and thoughtful enough to use some of rock's most unpleasant characteristics—its coarseness and primitivism, for example—in order to make sensitive and moving musical statements. As early as 1965 they were the heralds of rock's musical maturation, perhaps even more so than the Beatles. While the Beatles remained unbeatable for their eclectic virtuosity, as songwriters they were developing a stylistic versatility so completely successful that often the musical result was hardly recognizable as rock and roll. On the other hand, the Who were to make recordings of comparable sensitivity and musicality which remained undeniably rock-and-roll songs.

One might say that the Beatles were the first rock group to understand melody and its use in rock and roll, the Rolling Stones were the first to understand the social and political aspects of rock and roll as stylized and ongoing rebellion, while the Who (and a few other British groups) were the first to understand rock and roll formally, and to begin stripping rock music to its most essential elements, leaving an abstract musical and attitudinal framework within which there was room for almost endless invention and variation. There is, of course, a parallel between this distillation and abstraction of rock and roll and the simplicity of the blues, which imposes a severe and primitive discipline on the musician, yet still allows for considerable variation within rather a limited field.

As mentioned earlier many British musicians received a major share of their musical training playing in a number of blues bands which flourished in Britain in the sixties, chiefly under the leadership of Alexis Korner and John Mayall. The roster of musicians who played in the Korner or Mayall bands is a long one and includes many of the performers who were to figure prominently in rock and roll as the assault of the para-Beatle bands faded. Although Alexis Korner and John Mayall were both backwards-looking figures, trying as they were to graft an old black-American strain onto the British pop-music consciousness, the high standards of musicianship which they required from their players and their devotion to musical authenticity—though at times it seemed petty and niggling—produced a group of musicians who were both technically proficient and mentally prepared to play rock and roll with new levels of intensity and inventiveness.

The Yardbirds began as very much a blues band,

even to the extent of backing up the American blues singer and harmonica player Sonny Boy Williamson on his last European tour. However, they quickly abandoned the blues and, fired by a succession of the best British guitarists—Eric Clapton, Jeff Beck, Jimmy Page —turned out some of the most outstanding and musically shocking pop of their day: songs like "For Your Love," "I'm a Man," "Over Under Sideways Down" and others which brought a new level of virtuosity to pop music, principally in their guitar solos.

The Spencer Davis Group, a bit of a misnomer since the band's *raison d'être* was as a forum for the amazingly precocious talents of organist-guitarist-singer Stevie Winwood, were another rhythm-and-blues group who moved into the wider pop market and found success there. Their first hit record, "Gimme Some Lovin'," was a shocker at the time, with its mysterious and vaguely sinister heavily echoed vocal, over-loud and monotonous bass riff, and grinding Hammond organ. "Gimme Some Lovin' " offered a more visceral experience than most contemporary rock and foreshadowed the hyperamplified passions of Heavy Rock.

Singer-guitarist Donovan Leitch was in rather a different vein from most British performers. A folk singer cum rock and roller, his brand of musical Celtic mysticism foreshadowed California-bred flower power, and under the tutelage of British hit-maker Mickie Most, Donovan scored numerous chart successes.

Probably the most important of the immediately post-Beatles bands to emerge in Britain was Cream, who may be seen as capping a process of musical development which in the space of a few years transformed rock into a more serious, more emotionally trenchant, more inventive medium than it had been in 1963. Cream was a musicians' band. Their early repertoire comprised a sort of blues-jazz-pop pastiche which relied for much of its appeal on the pyrotechnic virtuosity of Cream's three members—Jack Bruce, Eric Clapton, and Ginger Baker—who were each reckoned to be the masters of their instruments. All three were blues and R&B veterans who had had some commercial success playing with pop groups—Clapton on the Yardbirds' first hit, Bruce with Manfred Manne, and Baker with the Graham Bond Organization. From the beginning their goal appears to have been to be a band in which each member was the musical equal of the others at the most rarified heights of pop music-making skill.

So Cream became the first "supergroup," the first rock band whose playing was so good that people were willing to hear the band go through extended solos and improvisations. One of the band's most popular songs was "Toad," an extended drum solo. Cream often used their songs just as a pretext for some rather free-form, jazzy music-making. Indeed, their songs were often merely brackets for the band's free-flying musicianship, helping to relate the band's playing, which was quite *outré* for the times, to the audience.

Most astonishing was Cream's incredible commercial success, which their songs—without catchy melodies and with mad lyrics (mostly by Pete Brown), with their self-indulgent and seemingly interminable soloing, with just about everything that made Cream different from other rock groups—would seem to militate against. Yet Cream were one of those bands who were so good and so different that even their inability to produce the contemporary pop shibboleths couldn't hold them back from popularity. More than any other rock group of the time, more than the Beatles or the Stones or the Who, Cream broke with the tradition of pop music. Their first album, *Fresh Cream,* was a bombshell, a red flag that signaled that there could never—that there *should* never—be a return to the safe and acceptable innocuousness of bland, three-minute pop tunes with pretty melodies.

That was the promise of Cream in 1966: a promise of liberation—not from commercialism, because after all Cream made far more money than most rock groups, but from the constriction and monotony of the three-minute pop song—and a promise of a new pop-music era in which free, unrestrained, savage music-making would be both financially acceptable to the music industry and aesthetically acceptable to the audience. This promise, like all good promises, went unfulfilled.

Although at the time Cream seemed to be just about the stunningest thing imaginable, so did the Hollies and the Animals and the Kinks and most other groups, so Cream didn't appear quite so forcefully as pop music's salvation. The atmosphere of the time wasn't really progressive or destiny-laden. There was not yet the feeling among pop-music adherents of being members of the chosen people and being herded toward the pastures of heaven by rock-and-roll shepherds. Rather, the prevalent mood was an almost mindless pleasure derived from being quite fortuitously one of the right people at the right time, at the cynosure of existence solely by virtue of youth and a taste for rock and roll. Sadly, this euphoria didn't last for long.

THE AMERICAN REACTION
1965-1967

• • •
GHOSTS OF THE HOOTENANNY ERA
• • •

America's pop-music reply to the Beatles-led British invasion of the hit parade was not long in coming, but it seemed like a semilifetime in teen-age terms. Although there may have been a certain nationalistic inspiration ("We'll teach them uppity Limies for beating us at our own game"), American pop music would probably have developed very much as it did, though perhaps not quite so rapidly, even without the Beatles to compete against. Purely urban East Coast responses to the Beatles met with a singular lack of success, and for a few years American rock and roll was to draw its chief inspiration from the dual vapidities of the folk boom and the West Coast life-style.

The folk boom, which began in the late fifties and continued into the mid-sixties, was one of the great American pop-music movements of the century. This craze for folk music may be seen as an almost inevitable response to the inanities of modern suburban American life. Folk music, even when commercialized and pasteurized by clean-cut no-talent hacks like the Kingston Trio, seemed to offer a deeper—though still pretty shallow—glance into the human soul than the pathetically jejune messages of the top ten.

Folk found most of its audience among American college students, and it should hardly be surprising that artistic pretention flowered lushly in so fertile a bed of aesthetic and intellectual bullshit as was the American college social scene of the late fifties. The commercial success of folk music was linked directly to American ideas about the necessity of a college education. The importance of a college education was inculcated in the mind of every young middle-class American from an early age, partly because Americans have the childish belief that every problem can be solved if only the potential solver has the right credentials and partly because a college education for all one's children was like a barbecue or a new Chrysler, just another suburban status symbol. So the legion of youth who had been packed off to college as proof of their parents affluence and faith in the American dream constituted an eager, almost rabid audience for the glib profundities of commercialized folk music.

The superstars of the folk era were the Kingston Trio, three wholesome and heartrendingly talentless young men; Harry Belafonte, who had a good voice and as a West Indian was obviously oppressed and deserving of a sympathetic audience; and Peter, Paul and Mary, who were unquestionably the best of a bad lot.

The folk boom took off in 1958 with the Kingston Trio's hit single "Tom Dooley," a rather low-key and monotonously compelling ballad about a fellow who was unjustly hanged in North Carolina in the nineteenth century—an exemplary folk tune which assuaged tepidly liberal consciences by wimpishly protesting a past injustice. Indeed, the American folk scene was so pervaded by earnest whinings about social justice that the term protest music was often used interchangeably with folk music.

The folk music boom occurred at the time of the mass white movement in the United States in support of equal civil rights for blacks. Unfortunately, the civil rights movement was nearly a century late in starting and so the sudden moral reawakening of white America may have been a little too conveniently conscience-soothing. Folk music was the Music of the Movement, and I have no wish to deprecate the courage or morality of those who were intensely involved in that movement. But whenever entertainment involves itself with politics the worthwhile and the meretricious become quite hideously mingled. It is thus appropriate to wonder how many of those who sang and listened to songs about equal opportunity, equal justice, and equal this and that were motivated more by fashion than by moral considerations.

Folk concerts were supposed to be hootenannies, performances where the audience was freely encouraged to participate by singing along, clapping and whatever other noisemaking activities they wished to indulge in, which all sounds like great fun. But in practice, folk concerts and the folk revival in general tended to be effortfully thoughtful, as everyone tried to be as intense and involved as possible so that his friends might remark: "My, how outstanding you are. How

morally pure, socially aware, and authentic you look."
Although at the same time artists like Pete Seeger were
creating sincere and socially responsible modern folk
music, the mass folk boom was as exciting as a boiled
potato and somewhat less substantial.

● ● ●
HORRORS, IT'S ART!
● ● ●

It's worth a not-so-brief digression to mention the popular American attitude toward art and art forms which
affected the folk boom. In the popular patriotic mythology, America is supposed to be a nation of responsible,
russet-coated, citizen-soldiers; Jeffersonians; the Ro-
mans of the New World—sober, pragmatic, and hard-
working.

When not working hard, Americans relax by having fun, which is any relatively mindless pursuit that
makes one feel good and laugh or at least chuckle. Fun
is what people have on Sunday afternoon at picnics or
outings. American advertisements quite often use fun
to sell their products when sex is thought to be inappro-
priate. Sex is neither work nor fun. Soft-drink advertisements rely particularly heavily on fun and often depict
orgies of fun that would make even a Nero among fun-
makers blush. They use hardcore fun like sack races,
pancake eating and frisbee throwing.

Now both fun and work eclipse art. Art is only for
the rich or homosexuals or Europeans, who are thought
to be both. Entertainment is fun, and whenever Americans mix entertainment and art you will find trouble
and a bit of the old *crise de conscience,* as Americans
just can't enjoy art. This is precisely what happened
with folk music, which attempted to mix entertainment

(fun) with art (must be pretentious) with yet another log for the pyre, politics. The folk musicians and fans sought to dignify and add substance to their music by making it increasingly and painfully artful and morally didactic. This just wasn't entertainment, sonny, this was serious business, and as happens whenever small minds set themselves to great tasks—be they artistic, moral or intellectual—tedium and pretention must follow.

There was, however, a perceptible rise in standards of folk connoisseurship as the Kingston Trio slipped in popularity and were replaced by the more talented Peter, Paul and Mary, who were in their turn followed by Joan Baez and Bob Dylan. The shift of popular opinion in favor of the better folkies coincided not too surprisingly with the dawning of the darkest era (obvious oxymoron) in modern American history. The twin horrors of the assassination of JFK and the Presidency of LBJ led folk musicians to find their subject matter in the problems of the present rather than the more shadowy injustices of the past. Folk music began to find authenticity in reality instead of mythology.

Bob Dylan was the outstanding personality to emerge from the tail end of the folk boom and become a major music talent. A Minnesota-born Jewish singer/songwriter, Dylan is considered by many to be the Prometheus of pop and certainly the most significant American pop performer. He is often called our leading poet by adoring fans and aging establishment critics who have just discovered rock and roll. Of course, Dylan is a poet in the sense that all pop lyricists are, but the term "poet" is not usually used when one talks about pop songwriters, just as it is not used to describe those who write advertising jingles for dog food and soap powder. When used to describe Dylan, the word "poet" has formal and panegyric connotations which derive from Dylan's lyrics being considerably more literary and obscure than most pop lyrics. Dylan loves words, understands them, and uses them well, and he is unquestionably one of the leading pop songwriters. Perhaps he is even the literary beacon of an illiterate audience, but T.S. Eliot he ain't.

Dylan deserted to the rock-and-roll camp at the 1965 Newport Folk Festival when he stunned and disappointed his fans by performing with an electric guitar—a very unfolklike thing to do—and was booed off the stage for "selling out." Since then he has gone through phases of using electric and nonelectric accompaniment, but he has remained clearly a rock musician.

Dylan's songs have been recorded by hundreds of other performers, and although the more extravagant claims as to the significance of his writing are insupportable, there is little question that he has written with great sensitivity at times and that by being more aware than most of the abstract value of words he generally raised the standards of pop lyricism.

Dylan's personal image is as important as his musical art because throughout his career, even though earning tremendous amounts of money (he earned £35,000—around $87,500—for his one-hour Isle of Wight performance in 1969), he has remained resolutely aloof from the show-business pop stardom establishment. Dylan has always been a low-key, somewhat drab, and mysterious figure who has retained something of the hopeful young folk singer who came to the Big Apple in 1961. Either he is a paragon of purity or his deliberate shunning of the flash and flamboyance of celebrity is meant to be a sign of his status as an artist instead of a pop star.

The most notable rock-and-roll followers of Dylan were the Byrds, the first American band to seriously challenge any of the British groups as exponents of the new rock. It's worth noting that the Byrds first tried to cash in on rock's new sound by releasing a pseudo-British single under the name the Beefeaters in 1964, but the following year they became very original and very American-sounding performers with their version of Dylan's "Mr. Tambourine Man." The Byrds were stars for the next two years and recorded some outstanding rock and roll, but as they became more musically adventurous and more heavily influenced by country-and-western music—which was not commercially hot with the teen-age audience at the time—they faded in popularity. The star of the Byrds was singer/guitarist Jim McGuinn, whose long, frizzed-out hair and tinted "granny" glasses caused a bit of a sensation. Indeed, the Byrds, though inspired by Bob Dylan and the eastern intellectual folk revival, were the first of the freaked-out West Coast bands. On their first national tour in 1965 they traveled with a support troop of California freaks, the most prominent of whom was a strange and hairy fellow who wore a cape and hopped about the stage in a fit of paralytic dervishry while the Byrds played. This proved a bit much for most audiences, though, and he and friends were shunted aside. The Byrds were the first rock group to show that a purely American sound could compete successfully with the Beatles and their followers.

• • •
NO MORE SURFIN'
• • •

Without question the Beach Boys, established long before the Beatles and still going strong, were the biggest American rock band. Before discussing the Beach Boys and their career, however, it's necessary to say something about the place of California in American culture.

Appropriately, California entered the American consciousness with the Gold Rush of 1849 and ever since has been the ceaselessly raped yet perennially virginal daughter of the nation. Almost every American thinks at one time or another about packing it in and going to California—the place is pretty, the climate's nice, and the grapefruit are good. The Spaniards, for all their centuries of occupation, were remarkably unsuccessful in establishing a dense highly developed colonial society in California, so the Americans who arrived in the post–Gold Rush years had a free hand in making the state a paradigm of the American Dream. California has remained that way: an original, adventurous, and tasteless land where nothing is out of place because everything is. And California treated its citizens well— at least the middle class, who prospered from the state's booming economy and built ranch houses with swimming pools and bought cars for their children. Californians were a different race: confident, crude, embarrassingly healthy. California teen-agers were equally unpleasant. Tanned, lithe, unacned, educated at massive campus-style high schools, they appeared to devote most of their time to sundry frolics of which surfing and hot-rodding were the most prominent and exciting.

The Beach Boys came out of this environment of sun, sand, high school, and hot rods with their 1962 hit record "Surfin' Surfari," which was quickly followed by "Surfin' USA" and "Surfer Girl." And the Beach Boys were not the only surf songsters in the charts. Jan and Dean, with "Surf City" ("two girls for every boy") and the Surfaris with "Wipe Out" were enjoying considerable success. The film industry had picked up on surfing a bit earlier and the beach-oriented California youth scene as early as 1959 with a ridiculous film called *Gidget*, but it was rock and roll that gave surfing and Californiaism their biggest boosts as the national youth crazes of the early sixties.

It seems curious that surfing should have become so popular when so few areas in the United States have the proper conditions for surfing. Part of it may have been due to the fact that the two states where surfing was most popular, California and Hawaii, were the last outposts of the American Dream. Or perhaps it was because surfing was a romantic and solitary sport pregnant with notions of man's struggle against the elements and the glory of individual achievement and various other inflated notions about a man proving his worth and a girl proving her worth by being with a man who's proved his worth. Surfing also offered an exotic and esoteric vocabulary that used words and phrases like "wipe out," "Ho daddy," "wahini," "woody," "baggies," and "hang ten." Finally, surfing was quite easy, as most people never got a chance to try it, especially if they lived in Akron or Tucson. So for the majority of American teens surfing was the ideal sport: it offered a culture that was attractive and indolent based around a sport that no one who lived in an area without regular six-foot waves could be expected to try.

Affluent and spiritually aimless societies often go through crazes of consumption and fads of all descriptions just as poor and spiritually oriented societies, medieval Europe for example, went through behavioral crazes of witch burning and public dancing. The modern American crazes like surfing or hula-hooping are activities in which people participate, and therefore make themselves less anonymous, by rushing off to buy some piece of specialized and overpriced fun-making gear. Just as postindustrialism has a tendency to make human relationships increasingly like commodity relationships, so it also transforms sport and recreation into a commercial activity where one need only buy the necessary equipment and do nothing more. Surfing and the craze for hot—meaning both fast and flashy—cars were both fads which betrayed more of a fascination with hardware and the accompanying social scene than with the actual sporting activity.

The Beach Boys' music was promoting two of the hottest fads in America. Almost all of their early songs were about either surfing or speeding around in hot rods, like "409" and "Little Deuce Coupe." Although only one of the Beach Boys, Dennis Wilson, was a hardcore surfer, they all looked the part with their short, blond hair, narrow chino pants and striped surfer shirts, or, on occasions when a dressier appearance was called for, clad in cheap continental-cut gabardine suits. The Beach Boys' great creative triumph was that while writing and performing songs whose subject matter was of the most imbecile nature ("New York's a lonely town when you're the only surfer boy around"), they were able to create music of some subtlety and complexity and evolved into one of the more interesting rock bands around. They even grew beards and smoked dope, but all that came later.

● ● ●
PSYCHEDELIC MADNESS
● ● ●

Although the surf boom was short-lived and declined steadily after 1965 it served to focus attention on California as the new hothouse of American musical production. The locational geography of pop music verges on the inscrutable, but there was a pronounced shift from the Middle Atlantic area, chiefly New York and Philadelphia in the pre-Beatles years, to California in the post-Beatles years.

The new musical capital of the U.S.—America's answer to Liverpool, as it was thought of—was San Francisco. San Francisco changed its image from the bordello-filled port of entry for the forty-niners to a city of some cultural pretention—a California version of a civilized East Coast city. (I've always thought that San Franciscans are bitter because they weren't born Bostonians.) The physical beauty of the city, its clement environment, and its generally tolerant attitude toward high culture turned it into a mecca for artists, writers, and beatniks in the nineteen fifties, but San Francisco remained most generally thought of as a picturesque but slightly out-of-it place until the emergence of the San Francisco Sound rock groups in 1965 and 1966.

In a flash, the city's hip community spawned a series of rock groups which began to dominate American pop music—the Jefferson Airplane, the Grateful Dead, Moby Grape, Quicksilver Messenger Service, and Big Brother and the Holding Company being among the most prominent. Although the San Francisco bands could hardly compete with both the British groups and certain other American bands in terms of chart success, they were important concert artists and album sellers. In addition, they introduced a new and highly original ethos into the pop scene simply because they were so uncompromisingly freaky and communally oriented.

The San Francisco scene is an example of the importance of entrepreneurial activity in the creation of pop culture. San Francisco had a large audience with a high proportion of college students and a considerable number of native rock musicians whose tasteless California-nouveau aesthetic was tempered by the precious intellectual precocity and affected cultural gentility of the city. But it lacked a forum for the right kind of artist-audience contact.

The gap was bridged by two local entrepreneurs: Chet Helms, who ran concerts at the Avalon Ballroom, and Bill Graham, who put on shows at the Fillmore. The Avalon and Fillmore concerts have often been compared to the New York avant-garde happenings of the fifties and sixties in which the environment became a part of the work of art rather than just a space in which to view a work of art (an interesting idea but, like so much of the avant-garde, tedious and nonsensical in execution). While the San Francisco concerts did not try to justify themselves formally and intellectually as the avant-garde happenings had, they were not only similar in concept, but much more successful in practice.

The audience became important participants in the concerts. The Fillmore and the Avalon were more than halls with stages; they were environments which provided a complete pop-music experience with their loudly amplified bands, fulgurating light shows and writhing rather than dancing audiences. Light shows, which were to become an important part of many rock concerts, were first introduced in San Francisco. They used strobe lights, colored lights, and lurid slides of sexually aroused amoebae and other strange things projected against the walls of the auditorium. These light shows were meant to re-create some of the visual and sensual experiences induced by taking LSD—in other words, they were psychedelic. Whether or not they succeeded is debatable: they certainly created a visual environment at rock concerts that was new and independent of older visual traditions. The San Francisco concerts relied extensively on poster advertising, and these posters, with their sinuous forms reminiscent of art nouveau and their original though virtually unreadable lettering, were the first graphic art style created by pop music. They were imitated in other parts of the United States and in other countries and were quite widely sold, decorating the walls of countless college dormitories.

The visual style of the San Francisco performers themselves was something of a novelty as well. They had much longer hair than any of the British rock and rollers (with the exception of a few aberrant and best-forgotten bands like the Hullabaloos), and the dress of performers and audience alike ranged from a drugged-out Gene Autry-cum-oil-rig-operator Western pastiche to the true psychedelic hippie look, which is how an intoxicated New Guinea tribesman given the run of your great aunt's wardrobe would dress.

Most important, the San Francisco bands were more communally aware than previous rock groups had been. It was difficult to distinguish visually between many of the San Francisco groups and the members of their audiences, and the popularity of drug-taking among both performers and audience linked them even more as social and legal outlaws.

● ● ●
THE NOBLE SAVAGE YES
● ● ●

The San Francisco scene introduced a new human type onto the world stage: the hippie or freak. Hippies were most easily distinguished by their extremely long hair; eclectic, multilayered, and berserkly polychromatic clothing; drug-taking; and a slangy and generally inarticulate style of speech. At first everyone with long hair was branded as a hippie by the "straights"—a term used to cover policemen, clergymen, parents, small-town newspaper editors, Republicans, hostile shop clerks, and most other people who were neither young nor with it—but the true hippie subculture flourished only in a few urban areas, most notably San Francisco's Haight–Ashbury district. The spin-off effects were felt everywhere, though, and there probably wasn't a single town in 1967–69 America without one long-haired, weird-looking druggie to serve as a local scapegoat.

Hippies could be pretty unpleasant characters. They did more to debase and corrupt the English language than any group with the possible exception of politicians and journalists. Their speech often consisted of little more than a string of bizarre catchwords and phrases like "far out," the eternally wondrous "wow," and the ubiquitous "man." It wasn't at all out of the ordinary to hear two hippies engaged in conversation with such dialogue as "Wow, like man did you, like, go to the concert last night man? Like it was really far out, man." "Oh, wow." So they usually weren't a very literate bunch. It's also true that they looked pretty unappealing, shunned work, bothered people for spare change, denied or ridiculed the fundamental precepts of American life, and in their own way could be a pretty brutal and dishonest lot. But in their completely negative approach to modern life, in their exaggerated, unrealistic and often hypocritical emphasis on the power of love to set everything right, they represented a devastating critique of the failure of the United States to provide a just and decent society. While it is true that the hippie movement was a farrago of laziness and stupidity wrapped in sanctimonious rhetoric about love, brotherhood, and human perfectability, the existence of the hippies and the widespread appeal of their life-style symbolized to many that something had indeed gone wrong with modern society. The hippies in no way provided an alternative to the society in which they found themselves, but they were the red spots that indicated a bad case of national spiritual measles.

The hippie movement fizzled as the Haight–Ashbury district and other hippie areas in cities like New York and Boston became squalid and crime-ridden. It may have been the drugs that did it, with their bodily destructiveness and social toxicism, but for whatever reason the true hippies just couldn't last. Although they were rationalized and mythologized into the twentieth century's equivalent of the Rousseauan natural man—the noble savage—as a group they possessed neither the intellectual equipment nor the primeval naïveté to play the role convincingly. While university-bound sociologists with liberal leanings extolled the praises of the hippies and envisioned the planting of a new garden of Eden by these children of love, ecstacy and hallucination, the hippie culture died in an agony of squalor and overdose.

● ● ●
WOODSTOCK NATION SELLS OUT
● ● ●

The hippies had a profound effect on American youth culture as a whole. Male hair became longer, clothes were wilder, drug use became more prevalent as kids got freakier. Part of this was the inherent appeal of weirdness and rebellion to youth, but much of it was due to increasing dissaffection from the American way. Although the trappings of hippie life were widely adopted abroad, the native American hippies had a particular intensity which derived from their protest against black oppression and against the continued slaughter and mutilation of American youth in Vietnam so that Lockheed might make a profit. The hippie was made a symbol of whatever anyone wanted to criticize in the U.S., whether it was a lack of patriotism or insufficiently strict discipline in Nebraska high schools. Like all the noble savages that had gone before, the hippies were something less than noble and something more than savage. Mostly they were just lost and confused, but their offer of a life based on instinct and sensuality rather than reason and economics was appealing. That love and reason should have been poised in opposition was sad, stupid, and unnecessary, but by their very outrageousness and the impracticality of their lives, the hippies became both the starting point and to an extent the focus of what became know as the Counter-culture.

The Counter-culture was meant to signify the maturity of the youth movement (pardon the oxymoron). No longer just a bunch of kids who dressed funny, wore their hair long, and jived to rock and roll, but a complete alternative society within the nation. Many saw the Counter-culture as the model for a new order on earth: a society of Edenic communities set in fields of organically cultivated vegetables, dedicated to love and peace . . . uggh! Of course it was never even remotely possible that American kids would abandon their Corvettes and color televisions for the more rustic delights of, say, New Jerusalem-on-the-Mississippi, but the idea of the Counter-culture was the inevitable product of idealism and idiocy set in the worsening economic and cultural milieu of late-nineteen-sixties America. The war in Vietnam was simultaneously being lost to the Communists and being revealed as a commercial and ideological charade. The increased alienation of one generation from another as extremes of dress and the use of drugs spread, and the vague feeling grew that life as lived by one's parents and as organized by the Nixons and Rockefellers was little more than an institutionalized and legalized system for the exploitation of the weak, the young, and the different. These were the facts of contemporary life that fueled the idea of the Counter-culture.

Of course disillusioned adults and idealistic children have always hoped that perhaps the younger generation might learn from the mistakes of the elder and build a better world, but for the first time in quite a while the sixties saw a younger generation who appeared to be irreconcilably different from their parents. The kids were stumbling forward with new art forms, paths to ecstacy, fashions, and political feelings. There are always differences between the generations in visual, aural, sartorial, and intellectual fashions, but this time pop culture had made a youth-oriented quantum leap, and it seemed as if the old folks would never catch up. The term "generation gap" was invented, used, and overused to describe this phenomenon. Everyone talked about the generation gap: it became the leading platitude of the times, much used by television commentators, rabbis, and child psychologists, but the generation gap was very real, painfully and generally destructive to the fabric of a society already weakened by the political and economic traumas of America's changing world role.

The Counter-culture, the hope that an alternative society might grow up and take over initiating a new golden age, was doomed from the start. Revolution was mooted by the trend-conscious at suburban cocktail parties and by the more radical and idealistic or idiotic young, and there was much talk of "when the revolution comes," but there was never a chance of revolution. Despite the masses of people who were motivated to march on Washington to protest the war in Vietnam, and despite the growth of red-hot radical groups like the Weathermen, there could never have been a revolution in the United States because there was neither sufficient mass support for drastic and irreversible change nor a sufficiently talented and credible elite to direct such change. But it all made for interesting chit-chat.

The Woodstock Art and Music Festival of 19 August 1969 was the orgasm of the Counter-culture, as about half a million kids sat, ate, slept, crapped, and fornicated through three days of rock music in a muddy field in upstate New York. To the music of a number of major rock groups—Jefferson Airplane; the Who; Santana; Crosby, Stills, Nash, and Young; and others—the audience lived its fantasy about the Counter-culture and it seemed to work. The occasion, while chaotic and dirty, was nonviolent, cooperative and suffused with the spirit of love. Whether the spirit of love and cooperation was spontaneous, self-conscious, or just an attempt by the audience to save the poorly organized festival from complete breakdown remains arguable, but the three days of peace and love were mythologized into the baptism of the "Woodstock Nation." Woodstock, we were told, proved that the Counter-culture was a viable idea. Three days of listening to rock-and-roll music under terrible conditions is hardly the equivalent of building and maintaining a new society. But people wanted to believe.

People wanted to believe that Woodstock was all sweetness, light, and good vibes. But the affair was tainted by the sordid commercial maneuverings of the festival's promoters who claimed to have lost a fortune in the service of the new order, but whose financial practices were questionable and who may have ended up with a substantial profit as the citizens of Woodstock Nation were fed a rapidly growing intake of Woodstock posters, tee shirts, record albums, and, yes, the film. The message that citizenship in Woodstock Nation was for sale was quite clear.

ROCK AT ITS ZENITH
1967-1972

• • •

THE NEW TRANSATLANTIC STYLE

• • •

Woodstock Nation's dreams of peace, love, and brotherhood among the young evaporated in December 1969 at a large free concert at Altamont, California. Three hundred thousand people arrived, hoping for a West Coast Woodstock and instead found themselves in a maelstrom of malice and misadministration which left four dead and many others shaken up by brawling and bad trips, and further disabused everyone of the notion that these kids could show the world a better way to live. The Jefferson Airplane performed at Altamont, witnessing the death of the culture that had created them, but it was even more fitting that the concert's headliners and instigators should be the Rolling Stones.

Altamont saw the triumph of no-nonsense old world rock-and-roll aggro over West Coast love, flowers, and all that jazz.

Not that the British bands had been unaffected by the American West Coast sound. Indeed, all the visual and philosophical claptrap from California was adopted with avidity and alacrity by the British bands, but tempered by distance and maybe even by the weather, the psychedelic style was little more than window dressing for the British rockers. The few, like Eric Burdon and the New Animals or Dantalian's Chariot, who tried seriously to emulate the West Coast sound never had a chance.

What the success of the American West Coast and psychedelic bands did to the British and to other American groups was to bring to rock lyrics some of the jargon of mysticism and more blatant references to the use of drugs, and to break down the structural simplicity of rock songs to a certain extent. West Coast bands had inured rock audiences to listen to extremely long and often ineptly played instrumental improvisations. In addition, the psychedelic scene's increasing preoccupation with Eastern, especially Indian, philosophy and life allowed the introduction of some new instrumental sounds, most notably the metallic drone of the sitar.

Rock and roll, admittedly, has never been particularly heavy on philosophy, and the increasing fascination with Indian and Chinese philosophy was little more than a trend-conscious groping for some exotic system of belief, which might, it was hoped, be more hospitable to Counter-cultural life-styles than conventional Western religions and philosophies. This constant turning of the young to mysticism and to the Orient, whether the product of profound introspection or mere trendiness and stupidity, certainly represented a substantial vote of no confidence in the dear old Judaeo-Christian tradition.

The three most important British bands—the Beatles, the Rolling Stones and Cream—were all affected by what had happened out in California. They started dressing more flamboyantly and exotically and became musically more adventurous. In 1967 the West Coast madness hit these three with a vengeance. The Beatles released *Sgt. Pepper's Lonely Hearts Club Band,* Cream released *Disraeli Gears,* and the Rolling Stones released *Their Satanic Majesties Request.* The first two were something more than hits, the last something worse than a miss. In all three cases, though, the bands who produced them were more freaked out, experimental, and exotic in both sound and appearance than they would have been without the inspiration of the San Francisco bands to goad them on.

Sgt. Pepper is arguably the finest rock album ever made, less arguably the twentieth century's most important piece of music and certainly not the paragon of man's artistic expressiveness. But the very fact that *Sgt. Pepper,* which is still just a rock-and-roll album, could be considered as perhaps one of the century's major musical accomplishments indicates both the rising intellectual status of rock and the increasing aesthetic validity of rock as a musical medium which could say more than "I love you baybee, oop wee ooh, ooh I do." *Sgt. Pepper* was tagged almost immediately as rock's first concept album.

While *Sgt. Pepper* shared with previous Beatle albums a unity of presentation done to the consistent excellence and virtuosity of the Beatles, it was the first rock album to have an overriding aesthetic design. The album was conceived as a complete and coherent musical entertainment composed of a series of pop songs. Although the individual songs which make up the album fail to relate to each other as clearly as, say, the movements of a symphony do, *Sgt. Pepper* is certainly far more than just a collection of brief tunes, as most rock albums were to continue to be.

The sound of the album was lush, orchestral, multilayered—a shock and a surprise as the Beatles broke from the constraints of a rock band sound with an orchestral backing and successfully integrated a multiplicity of instrumental and noninstrumental sounds.

As the Beatles began to spend more time working in the studio and less time performing in concert, their musical productions became more sophisticated and subtle, less geared to wringing the last orgasmic yelp out of eleven-year-old girls in concert halls. Both *Rubber Soul* and *Revolver,* the two albums which immediately preceded *Sgt. Pepper,* were more complex, musical, and intelligent than the band's earlier recordings, but they were still not adequate warning for *Sgt. Pepper*'s radical innovation.

But the Beatles in their *Sgt. Pepper* and post–*Sgt. Pepper* phases are a problem, as much of their material began to sound like something other than rock and roll. How could the vaudevillian sound of a cut from *Sgt. Pepper* like "For the Benefit of Mister Kite" possibly be related to the explosive cacophony of the Who or the strident punkiness of the Rolling Stones' "Get Off of My Cloud"? It seemed as if rock and roll was beginning to tear apart musically as it reached its greatest artistic achievements.

What kept rock and roll together through those years, when one rock song would have a brass band and another would have five overamplified guitars, was the spongelike aesthetic quality of the medium. Rock and roll could soak up almost any musical influence and fatten on it because rock and roll is rather more than music—it is a way of understanding and listening to music; it is a way of living; it is a way of relating performer to audience to artistic creation to world that shuns formal rigidities. Rock and roll is an art that is almost completely predicated on eclecticism and aesthetic promiscuity. It is a libertarian as well as a commercial art, and that is why the music and the audience can thrive on both garbage and ambrosia.

From the time of *Sgt. Pepper* on, the Beatles stood outside the mainstream of rock. They continued to produce hit singles until their breakup in 1970, but they had transcended rock and roll: they were the gods who looked down from Olympus when the fancy struck them and occasionally meddled in the affairs of lesser beings when it would amuse them. After *Sgt. Pepper* the Beatle's breakup was ineluctable artistic necessity if any one of them ever wanted to play rock and roll again—they had just gone too high.

The Rolling Stones were in sharp contrast. Their album of 1967, *Their Satanic Majesties Request,* was ambitious, eclectic, mystical, and an abject failure. Suffice it to say that *Their Satanic Majesties Request* was rubbish and that, happily, since then the Rolling Stones have been rock and rolling in less pretentious and far better style.

Cream's *Disraeli Gears* was quite a step ahead of their debut album. Shunning the blues orientation of their earliest work, Cream created one of the few classic electric rock albums. The forcefulness of Ginger Baker's drumming, the particular lyricism of Jack Bruce's singing and bass playing, and the complex savagery of Eric Clapton's guitar work catapulted Cream into the vanguard of contemporary rock groups. They also scored their first American hit single with "Sunshine of Your Love," a song taken from the *Disraeli Gears* album. It was the song of the times. It had lyrics that were weird, romantic, and drug-inspired, it had a heavy bass riff, it had beautifully bizarre wah-wah guitar playing. It had everything. Cream even made the fashion change from leather and army-surplus–clad British bluesmen to flower-shirted frizzed-hair freaks.

While the major British rock groups were absorbing and transmuting the California freak ethos, a young American guitarist named Jimi Hendrix was almost spontaneously generated as rock and roll's new super idol. Hendrix had received his musical training in a number of American soul and R&B groups and after being discovered by a British entrepreneur—Chas Chandler, former bass player with the Animals—went to Britain to put together a backing band and record. His first album, *Are You Experienced?* and a hit single from it, "Purple Haze," established Hendrix as one of the most extraordinary performers in the recent history of pop music. His technical skill and the almost gymnastic virtuosity of his guitar playing were and remain unrivaled. While both his singing and his song writing ability were terribly inconsistent, his exploitation of the many sound possibilities of the electric guitar placed him far above most rock musicians.

It was the extramusical factors in his make-up, however, that made Hendrix a colossus, for he was the superspade, every white American's vision of black sexuality incarnate, and more. He was the cultural virtuoso of the times—the drugged-out, dressed-up, hyperphallic hipster. He was a musical internationalist, for his music was an amalgam of British and American styles. While Hendrix could be a sensitive and lyrical musician, much of what he played on stage and in the recording studio was noisy, self-indulgent junk, but he was always real rock and roll. Hendrix was sexy, tasteless, nasty, flamboyant; he was a performer whose personality was perhaps the major part of his artistic creation.

Hendrix went from strength to strength at first, but his music and his personality became increasingly chaotic. His death in 1970 was hardly a surprise. The music and the artist had that certain intensity that one only finds in those who live at the edge of existence. Hendrix had recorded a prodigious amount of music, and five years after his death new albums were still being released. Rock and roll doesn't transcend mortality so much as it makes it seem irrelevant: without the knowledge that Hendrix is there to perform, his recordings, however brilliant, seem faded and vapid. Hendrix was a performer of such vitality that his art could not outlive him.

And so with Janis Joplin, the Texas-born blues-rock singer who began her career with San Francisco's Big Brother and the Holding Company. Joplin was an outrageous personality—a bit of a tart, a boozer, a singer of incredible power and expressiveness who, even though hampered by a lack of good material and an extremely lame backing band, became one of the few female rock-and-roll idols. She finally left Big Brother, got together a new band, and did a fair amount of recording with them, but she died of a drug overdose in a motel room in the autumn of 1970. Janis too has begun to fade from memory.

Interestingly enough, both Joplin and Hendrix first rose to prominence in 1967 at the Monterey Pop Festival, which could probably be thought of as Woodstock's grandfather. They represented a new wave of pop-music talent. Educated by the Beatles and the other

British rockers, influenced but not suffocated by the West Coast sound, Joplin and Hendrix were two uncompromisingly individual and independent performers. Of the two, Hendrix was more important and influential, but they both satisfied rock and roll's growing demand for more style intensity and originality than the established British and the West Coast bands could offer. It all began in 1967—annus mirabilis—the year of Hendrix and Joplin, the year of Cream's ascension and the Beatles' apotheosis, the year the Rolling Stones got smart.

Alongside the Counter-culture, which was born in San Francisco and checked out at Altamont, there was this new trend in rock and roll. Rock became more mature, more sure of itself as an art which was strong enough to withstand the most brutal and crude sentiments yet sophisticated enough to offer more than just pop songs. The British invasion of 1964 had been repelled by an American rally whose fortress was California, and a new transatlantic consensus was the result. From the late sixties on, rock and roll was less timid, less provincial, perhaps, in its growing artfulness and complexity, somewhat less sensitive and authentic. The Trimurti of energy, outrage, and money ruled with a firm hand.

• • •
BAROQUE AND ROLL
• • •

Rock was in its age of excess, a period in which the darker, more visceral aspects of the art were distilled and often grotesquely amplified. This was the realization of all that the most basic aspects of rock had aspired to: the time of Heavy Rock, Downer Rock, Witch and

Warlock Rock, Fascist Rock, phweeped and zaarked Techno Rock. Rock bands and performers became more distant from their audiences, more theatrical and on stage. Rock discovered Hollywood and seventeenth-century Rome simultaneously.

The hippie experience had made the rock audience both more aware of pure bodily thrills and attuned to the supernatural—countervailing tendencies on the surface but linked by a distrust of reason and intellect and by the premium both placed on direct and intense experience. People were receptive to what became known as Heavy Rock: loud, forceful, clearly rhythmical rock made technically possible by improvements in amplification—to produce the required sound levels—and commercially possible by the changed audience climate of opinion. Heavy Rock was the great pop-music innovation of the late sixties. Heavy Rock was to rock and roll what rock and roll had been to earlier pop music: Neanderthal, atomic sledgehammer stuff.

Cream gave off intimations of heaviness in much of their concert performances and on the "live" two-disc album *Wheels of Fire,* but the band's often jazzy and disintegrative tendencies militated against their becoming a true Heavy Rock band. Cream, with their personal and musical wrangles which eventually led to their breakup, just didn't have the extreme amount of musical cohesion that Heavy Rock requires. *Wheels of Fire* did contain some of the best music of the year, though.

It was another British band, Led Zeppelin, who brought the first authentic Heavy Rock to the world and went on to become one of the most successful and exciting rock bands ever. Zeppelin grew out of the wreckage of the Yardbirds when that band's last lead guitarist, Jimmy Page, teamed up with arranger-bassist John Paul Jones and two musicians from a Birmingham rock group—singer Robert Plant and drummer John Bonham. The new group was going to perform under the old Yardbirds name, but the Who's drummer, Keith Moon, suggested they call themselves Led Zeppelin— even less flightworthy than a led balloon (ha-ha). There were five weeks of rehearsal; an album was recorded and released in early 1969. Since the release of that first unprepossessing album, *Led Zeppelin,* the band has sold perhaps fifteen million albums.

Led Zeppelin were loud, basic, perhaps even primitive. All of them were outstanding musicians: Jimmy Page is, with the possible exceptions of Eric Clapton, Jimi Hendrix or Ritchie Blackmore, the definitive rock-and-roll guitarist. Notwithstanding the choreographed eroticism of Mick Jagger, Robert Plant is rock and roll's best vocal performer.

From "Good Times, Bad Times," the first cut on their first album, Led Zeppelin established themselves as a band who could take rock in new directions. Although some of their material had a definite blues orientation, they were not merely a second-generation blues band. Equally, they were not pop-song makers: they didn't even release a single. They shunned publicity and little was and is known about their private lives. Their musical power alone raised them to stardom. The quality of their recorded work has been uneven: their second album a masterpiece, their third album a dud, the others varying in quality. At the start of their career they seemed to fill a power vacuum left by the recently broken-up Cream, and they rivaled the Jeff Beck Group —led by another former Yardbird guitarist—for the largest share of the hard blues-rock market.

Yet Zeppelin and their music were more subtly

original and seductive than they first appeared. They had unrivaled emotional impact but at the same time wrote and played with amazing sophistication and delicacy. Their most famous composition, "Stairway to Heaven," is probably the best rock song ever recorded.

But the superficial aspects of Led Zeppelin—the high volume, the strong, simple rhythm and basic song structures—inspired a horde of bands, some rather good, others incredibly bad (the heavy metal groups in particular—an army of impotent musical rapists).

America's leading Heavy Rock group was Grand Funk Railroad, a hard-rocking, terrifically exciting, and sometimes terribly bad trio who seemed to be hyperboled into stardom by their manager, Terry Knight, but who later proved themselves capable of producing some palatable though not necessarily delicious music.

Heavy Rock provided the ultimate in musical escapism. It is so emotionally and physically exhausting and sometimes painfully loud that one doesn't really have the energy or inclination to think of much other than the music. All through the sixties rock had been getting heavier, but Heavy Rock took hold of the U.S. audience at a particularly troubled time in history—the early Nixon years: the years of nearly ubiquitous protest against the conduct of the war in Vietnam; years of tortured national conscience-twisting which climaxed, but didn't culminate, in the killing of some protesting students at Kent State University in the spring of 1970.

It appeared that society had formally declared war against the young, and Heavy Rock brought forth Downer Rock, a particularly appropriate genre for the times. Downer Rock may be described as superamplified, usually badly played, simplistic rock with a mystico-morbid message. Downer Rock's chief exponents were Black Sabbath, a thuggy, atavistic, and philosophically lugubrious British quartet who became quite successful performing songs about paranoia, World War III, and other whistle-a-happy-tune subjects. The American kings of Downer Rock were Bloodrock, who had a big hit called "DOA." Yucch . . . All very distasteful and unusually unconstructive. MC5, a band from Detroit, Michigan, were almost in a class of their own. Amazingly inept, bunglingly frantic, their lyrics were mostly childishly revolutionary cant; their music sounded like the hum of a faulty toaster amplified ten thousand fold. They enjoyed some popularity and then mercifully melted back into Motor City.

Aside from Grand Funk and a few others, it was the British who dominated the Heavy Rock field, whereas the most interesting American bands were in a softer mold. Crosby, Stills, Nash, and Young, formed by veterans of a few prominent rock groups (the Hollies, the Byrds, Buffalo Springfield) made their debut at Woodstock and could sing some pretty good and every now and again some pretty awful songs. They became very big, with their country-and-western–influenced close vocal harmonizing, but were always breaking up, reforming, and in general appearing to be quite confused.

Among the most promising American groups to see the light in the heavy metal haze of crap like the Amboy Dukes and the Electric Prunes were the Allman Brothers Band and the Creedance Clearwater Revival. The Allman Brothers were good ole boys from the South whose major asset was the extraordinary guitar playing of Duane Allman. The band performed competent and occasionally exciting blues rock with a Southern inflection, toured ceaselessly, and became quite successful and increasingly something more than just a good band.

Creedance Clearwater Revival are a special case. A

San Francisco Bay area band, they kicked around for years until scoring a major hit in 1968 with an old Dale Hawkins song, "Suzie Q." CCR were a superbly simple band who played almost archaic, unadorned, solid rock and roll. Their mastermind was guitarist-producer-singer-dictator John Fogerty, who wrote all the band's material. Creedance recorded a string of hits and became, quite unspectacularly, the most successful American rock group ever. Much of the band's success was due to Fogerty, a mediocre lead guitarist by any standards, but an exciting and distinctive singer and songwriter with an uncanny understanding of what made a hit record. Given the magnitude of their success, there is surprisingly little to say about Creedance Clearwater. They were a most workmanlike band who played well, recorded good and plain rock songs, and made a lot of money. CCR and the Allman Brothers were a simple and refreshing interlude.

The turn of the decade was a boom period for rock, and even though (with the exception of the two groups just mentioned) Heavy Rock and its little brothers dominated the field, there was an amazing efflorescence of adventurous and interesting, if not always good, rock groups and musical styles. Rock was a more confident medium than ever before, making more money, mustering more intellectual and critical support, and broadening its base of operations, as it were. As the distance between performers and audience widened, the cultural supply lines became a bit attenuated, but they were not yet too long.

The British were in the forefront of rock experimentation and eccentricity. Former Spencer Davis Group whizz-kid Stevie Winwood, after an unfortunate interlude with ex-Cream members Ginger Baker and Eric Clapton in a band named, with unusual candor,

Blind Faith, re-formed Traffic (his pre-Blind Faith band) and began recording. Traffic were what might be called an Art Rock band. They were softer than most groups, used keyboard and wind instruments regularly, and drew much musical capital from jazz, classical music, and the English folk tradition rather than from rhythm-and-blues or country-and-western music as most rock bands did. Traffic had an interesting and troubled career, with numerous breakups and personnel changes, and they are notable as the first British rock band to rent a cottage in the country to rehearse and "get it together." The practice became so popular that for a time it appeared that the only inhabitants of the more picturesque parts of the British landscape would be cottage-dwelling rock musicians. Fortunately for continued agricultural production, that wasn't to be the case; at any rate, Heavy Rock could never have become a cottage industry, while Art Rock could.

Some Art Rock bands were heavily influenced, sometimes to the point of plagiarism, by classical music and "serious" modern composers. Among the more literate, far out, and pretentious Art Rock groups were Procol Harum, the Nice, and Pink Floyd. Some of them put a premium on technical proficiency (the Nice), others on obscure and meaning-laden lyrics (Procol Harum), others on funny noises (Pink Floyd). A heterogeneous bunch, including as they did such dissimilar bands as the Soft Machine (keyboard-centered, hyper-energetic, free form) and Fairport Convention (well-scrubbed, whole-grain, rural rock and roll), the Art Rockers made some good and often great music and encouraged the mainstream rock bands to be more daring.

The years 1968 to 1972 also witnessed a major

change in pop music, as for the first time in some years solo performers began to be accepted once again by the pop audience. Solo artists had dominated pop music before the coming of the Beatles ("I tell ya, four guys with guitars aint got a chance") but fell into disfavor with the popularity of the group format. The emergence of bands which were essentially one-man shows —the Jimi Hendrix Experience, for example—made audiences more receptive to the idea of solo performers once again, but the renascence of solo artistry was ushered in by Simon and Garfunkel (I know, it sounds like a duo) and by the recordings of the individual former Beatles. A solo artist may, of course, perform in a band format, but there is no question about who's running the show and who the audience has come to see. The rise to prominence of the solo artists again may be a consequence of the growing pressure on the rock performer to be a much-larger-than-life superstar: the age of Baroque requires the age of absolutism.

Paul Simon of Simon and Garfunkel was an archetypal singer-songwriter performer, a type influenced into existence by Bob Dylan, one of the few solo artists to withstand the onslaught of groups. Simon recorded and performed for many years with Art Garfunkel, splitting to go officially solo in 1970, but throughout the Simon and Garfunkel partnership there was never any doubt that Simon was the duo's chief attraction. Simon wrote scores of songs, had an excellent grasp of melody and lyric, and wrote one of the very few rock classics, "Bridge Over Troubled Waters," which has probably been recorded by more performers than any modern pop song. Simon has always stood outside out of the rock-and-roll mainstream, and although some of his early work was tiresome and pretentious, he is one of pop music's most significant and best songwriters. Like Dylan, he has avoided the flash and publicity overkill of garden-variety rock stardom.

All four Beatles were quick to release solo albums after the band broke up owing to personal differences, but it was only George Harrison—who had been stifled so long by the overwhelming songwriting talents of Lennon and McCartney—and Paul McCartney who succeeded in recording appealing and admirable albums at the beginning of their solo careers.

The main trends—Heavy Rock, Downer Rock, Art Rock, and solo artists—aside, the pop scene was pullulating with new bands and performers. Chicago and Blood, Sweat, and Tears, two rock-and-roll big bands with horns and everything, became successful, each with their own brand of insipid schmaltz. The Band, a countrified rock group who had backed up Dylan on occasion, were recognized as worthwhile performers in their own right.

The breakup of the Small Faces, who recorded some of the best British rock of the sixties, produced two new bands: the Faces and Humble Pie. Humble Pie had an uneven career, recording some brilliantly good stuff and, due to the writing difficulties that followed the departure of composer-guitarist Peter Frampton, some pretty ordinary tunes.

The Faces were to become major stars as the leading practitioners of a style most aptly described as rhythm and booze—good humored, energetic bashing in the old rock style. The Faces looked good, played tolerably well, and were fronted by one of rock's most exciting performers, vocalist Rod Stewart, who looks rather like a rooster just pulled out of a vat of whisky. While the Faces are hardly innovators, they have consistently and cheerfully produced good old rock and roll, and I hope that they will continue to do so.

A few of the products of the British blues boom enjoyed brief and belated success in the United States at the same time, particularly John Mayall and Fleetwood Mac, a band led by a former Mayall guitarist, Peter Green. Green left Fleetwood Mac at the height of their success, working in turn as a grave digger and a hospital porter, but before retiring he recorded some extraordinary tracks, most notably "The Green Manalishi."

The list of rock performers who came into the light, made money, and then plodded on or disappeared in those years is a long one: the Doors (briefly the world's highest-paid rock act), the Flying Burrito Brothers, Free, Colosseum, Delaney and Bonnie, Iron Butterfly, Joe Cocker, Vanilla Fudge, King Crimson, Love, the Nazz—enough, enough, arrggh, stop. Whew. They were boom years and there was a wondrous growth of rock groups to satisfy a hungry market.

While many of the old rock bands exhausted themselves or grew too prosperous or quarrelsome and broke up, the Rolling Stones and the Who remained the strongest link with the early days. After the disastrous *Their Satanic Majesties Request,* the Stones returned to their simpler, bluesy punk-rock style and turned out three of the great rock albums in three years: *Beggars Banquet, Let It Bleed* (probably their best), and *Sticky Fingers.* The world of rock is a fickle and trend-conscious one, and the devotion and constancy of the Rolling Stones' fans, as well as the cohesion and durability of the band itself, are the most telling indications of the special place that the Stones occupy in contemporary rock and roll.

The Who reached new levels of success and wide acceptance with *Tommy,* a "rock opera" written by

Pete Townshend, which was first performed in 1969 and subsequently (1975) made into a film. The success of *Tommy* was surpassed by the Tim Rice and Andrew Lloyd Weber rock opera *Jesus Christ Superstar,* a smash hit which was staged in London, New York, and many other cities, filmed, and recorded a few times. Both *Tommy* and *Jesus Christ Superstar* are worthwhile and entertaining works, but as attempts to establish rock and roll as the high-culture musical mode of our time by transforming an old and culturally significant musical form into a vehicle for the presentation of pop tunes, they are something of a charade and a dead end. Rock and roll is good enough to stand on its own and to create its own forms without resorting to the pretention of using archaic musical forms that have been sanctioned as fine art in an effort to gain further respectability for itself. The Who followed *Tommy* with *Who's Next,* their best album.

A few other bands had the staying power of the Rolling Stones and the Who, among them the Moody Blues, a sensitive and at times too-precious British rock group who have been consistent hit-makers and who developed into a band of considerable originality with their lush semiorchestral and ersatz-Wagnerian style.

The most obvious indication of the adventurous mass taste of the years 1968 to 1972 was the commercial success of Jethro Tull. Fronted by singer-flautist Ian Anderson, Tull's music was an amalgam of Heavy Rock, jazz, classical, and folk inspiration—about as eclectic as one could get. Much of the band's initial success must have been due to Anderson's extravagant stage performance—dressed like a demented escapee from a convalescent home for superannuated street freaks, he would hop about the stage on one leg and tell jokes between songs—but the large number of records that Tull sold must be an indication that people liked the band's music as well as their stage act. Tull's music was adventurous, powerful, and refreshing stuff; their second album, *Stand Up,* compares favorably with any other rock album, and Anderson was a temerarious musical innovator. The band's fourth album, *Thick As a Brick,* was a continuous piece of music, but unfortunately often tedious and obscure. Tull's later work didn't equal the quality of their first recordings, and under an at times merciless critical barrage, Anderson has frequently "retired" from pop-music activity, but Jethro Tull at their best were one of the more original and innovative bands around.

That Jethro Tull, Creedance Clearwater and Black Sabbath could all be successful at the same time says much about audience receptiveness and the aesthetic flexibility of the times. The turn of the decade was perhaps the zenith of rock and roll: a time when people were willing to relax their musical prejudices, to experiment with their purchases of records and concert tickets, and to listen to musical experimentation, some of which (like Jethro Tull's) led to interesting places, while other bands (like the Flock) found only new dead-end streets to explore. Perhaps because the world seemed unusually hostile in those days, the young audience had more of an interest in creating their own aesthetic and cultural world based around rock and roll. For all its excesses, it was a comfortable and confident time, like the garden-party summers of pre-1914 Europe. A time when the rabid fanaticism of the early Beatle years and the mindless philosophizing of the West Coast period had both been tempered by age and commercial success. Rock and roll was neither fighting for its survival nor yearning for social and economic justification. Rock-and-roll culture had come to terms with the world. For a brief while there was aesthetic pluralism and experimentation and a willing audience to provide support and encouragement.

ROCK-AND-ROLL FACTS,
MYTHS, AND LEGENDS

• • •
THE STARS AND THEIR SYSTEM
• • •

It is a truism created by Hollywood press agentry and sustained by postindustrialism that the people—God bless 'em—need stars to sprinkle a bit of fairy dust on their drab lives. This is partly true, but for whatever reason we have them, stars figure prominently in rock and roll and one can discern a pattern of rock history of sorts by looking at the evolution of rock-star style.

Rock failed to consolidate its hold on the feverishly hebetudinous imagination of American teendom until its first twenty-four-carat star in the person of Elvis Presley arrived on the scene. Presley was Hollywood-style flash, pastel Cadillacs (one for each day of the week), gold lamé suits: real glam stuff much more likely to sink its grappling hooks into the popular mind than the frantic sharkskin-suited inner-city jive bombers and the garish yahoo cornpone pudginess of Bill Haley and the Comets. Presley was a great rock singer, moved his hips the right way, and had good songs to sing, but it was the box rather than the added vitamins that sold his corn flakes. And of course he made the transition from rock star to movie star without too many scars to show for it.

But Presley was a hard act to follow, and the rock-and-roll establishment was unable to produce a figure of comparable magnetism and appeal for many years after. They didn't stop trying, though, and a succession of simpering greaseballs who occasionally produced hit records and usually came from Philadelphia were presented to the public with perverse relentlessness on record and on *American Bandstand*. Mostly, the immediately post-Presley era was a time of either superficially attractive one-hit wonders or dependable hitmakers like Dion and the Belmonts, who made records that were good to dance to but failed to attract much interest in their creators as personalities worthy of concern or emulation. So although rock and roll aesthetically had a lot of aboveness in those days, that is, the musical styles were handed to the audience by writers and performers, the teen-age rock-and-roll life-style had a lot of belowness, that is, the fashions and the way of life were grassroots creations. Even though the moguls tried, they just couldn't make stars out of Bobby Vee, Fabian, and company—the kids were buying, but only the records, not really the performers. There were touches of fan hysteria every now and again but it just didn't last. Even Buddy Holly, possibly the greatest of rock and rollers, just didn't have what it takes to be a true star. There wasn't much action on the star front until the British arrived.

The Beatles and the Stones were the first new rock-star figures. They were cute, a bit weird, exotic, musically startling, appealing in every conceivable way—the perfect receptacles for every teen-ager's fantasies about everything. They seemed so independent of the American way and so innovative in terms of fashion and music, so different from what had come before, that they were tailor-made for stardom. Hysterical adulation equaling or exceeding that which had been accorded to Elvis was focused on the Stones and the Beatles. Fans wanted to know everything about their new darlings. Did Mick like chopped liver? How tall was Paul's mother? Did Ringo believe in transubstantiation? If nothing else, stars are a safety valve for the public's prurience. Be they rock musicians, baseball players, or actors. People have to know just everything about their current heart throbs.

The British bands were pure star stuff and they knew it. They made scads of money and blew it in the right ways: Charlie Watts, probably the most pedestrian of the Rolling Stones, set a new trend by being the first rock star to buy a country house. All the better British bands, but particularly the Stones and the Beatles, were shrieked at, cried over, and prized for their charming personalities as much as for their music. It was all in the good old show biz tradition of *Silver Screen* and *A Star Is Born.*

Sadly, the American groups who came out of the West Coast scene put an end to such delightful nonsense. They were too drugged out, aware, and part of the community, man, to tolerate having little girls build reliquaries for locks of their hair or dirty hotel towels they had used. They were too purposeful, serious, and politically motivated for that sort of crap. They failed to realize that that sort of crap is great fun.

Stardom seemed to be leaving the rock scene as stars gave way to earnest music-makers. Bands like Led Zeppelin and Deep Purple seemed to shun the trappings of stardom, and although they were among the most popular performers on the pop scene, their lives in public seemed to begin and end on stage. Nonetheless, most postpsychedelic performers, especially the British ones, brought stardom back with a vengeance. Performers like Elton John, whose bizarre, extravagantly ostentatious, and often tasteless life-style fits into the star mold which demands that performers be bigger, if not necessarily better, than life.

The post-1969 Baroque stage of tortured stylized Heavy Rock and ever more pretentious Art Rock was, as we have noted, also an age of absolutism, of increased emphasis on the cultural prepotency of the individual rock musician. Although fans no longer worried about what Star X's pet peeves were, everyone knew who all the members of any of a number of bands were. It became important to recognize the contribution of each individual to the group. People began to be aware of guitar virtuosi and who the best drummers were. This may indicate increased public awareness of the musical art in rock and roll, but the cult of individualism which this awareness fostered among rock musicians may have egged many on to excesses of self-indulgence. Groups became less cohesive units for collective music-making and more just pretexts for individual show-offs. Pretty soon everyone in rock and roll became a star of sorts.

There was a spillover effect as stardom became banal, the commonplace condition of all in the rock world. Producers became stars and managers became stars and guys who carried amplifiers became stars. Everyone tried to catch a suntan in the reflected glories of the popular idols. An increased amount of attention was given to all varieties of camp followers and hangers on. Groupies became an especially hot topic. Groupies are women who rather indiscriminately dispense their favors to rock musicians and associates: sexual pop fans. Eric Clapton said something about groupies fucking names and not people.

The groupie scene was, like rock and roll itself, more concerned with lust than love. There was quite a lot of misplaced indignation about groupies linking them with degeneracy among youth and the ultimate downfall of everything that we hold sacred. All quite nonsensical, really. Promiscuity is hardly a twentieth-century innovation, and some women have always had definite vocational preferences in their choice of men: army groupies, political groupies, and so on. Sad perhaps for some of those involved, but really quite harmless and surely conducive to good morale among the troops. As for those stories about sexual congress with salamis and what not, they are no doubt true and acceptably kinky, but who really knows what went on in Napoleon's tent at night? Groupies are interesting because sex makes for good reading, but they are really only important to rock and roll in a minor way as fans who needed extremely close contact with their favorite stars.

There may be just too many rock stars; but few have the talent or flash of Elton John, and at times the genre appears to have become too star-studded. Soon even the fans will be stars. Paradoxically, as stars proliferated, true cases of fan hysteria became rare, and until quite recently there was little of the Beatlemania-style fainting and knicker-wetting. That is, until a few colossally talentless bands like the Bay City Rollers came along and began to cause some of the old hysteria among younger rock fans.

If anything, the percolation of stardom away from the center of rock and roll and down to the cousin of what's-his-name-the-guitarist with the who-are-they's is a good thing. It cheapens the concept of stardom, but, after all, stardom is a pretty cheap concept anyway. So everyone might as well be a star, and, after all, who cares what Paul McCartney's favorite color is?

● ● ●
THE ROCK ESTABLISHMENT
● ● ●

Rock and roll is a commercial as well as an aesthetic undertaking. A pop musician can't be a pop musician without an audience: there are no rock stars sitting in attics playing to the rafters. Changes in the nature of artistic patronage in the last two centuries—changes brought on by mass education and mass affluence— have caused artists and musicians to rely on a mass of patrons (the buyers of their cultural commodities) rather than on an oligopoly of wealthy potentates of refined taste. It is axiomatic in a capitalist society that one must earn a living: one earns money by selling either skills or the products of one's labor. The rock and roller earns money by selling his music to the public, and so we must have a music marketplace, a zone where the public and the performer meet and exchange money for entertainment. The music marketplace is national and international rather than local in scope, so the means by which the commodity—music— is distributed to the public must be organized on a large scale. The means of distribution in the rock-and-roll economic world are radio, concerts, recordings, television, films—all the communications media which can present an artist and his creation to the public.

These means of distribution are massive—requiring a skilled body of organizers, bureaucrats, and entrepreneurs to organize and service them—and costly to maintain, which means that access to them must be restricted to those who in the judgment of the bureaucrats, organizers, and entrepreneurs stand the greatest chance of being favorably received by the public and so paying the cost of presenting them and of course a profit to boot. There are a large number of performers seeking stardom, or at least success; most of them are rotten, and the number of new acts that the means of distribution can accept is limited, so decisions must be made about who will have a chance to reach the public. These decisions are made regularly by radio programmers who decide which recordings to play, concert promoters who decide which performers to sponsor in concert tours, and record company execs who decide which acts to sign to their labels. With so many people of varying and often doubtful qualifications involved, mistakes must be made: some performers will be on ice for years before getting a chance to make good, and others will never even get that chance.

The link between the performer and the distributors is the manager, the man who is meant to pilot rock acts to success. The manager is almost by definition in a constant jam: he must empathize personally and artistically with his artists yet at the same time be able to conceive of them in commercial terms as marketable product and plan his management strategy accordingly. The artist-manager relation is crucial to the success of any performer, since good management can open doors, grease the ways, or salvage a foundering career. Good management is skill and understanding, though—not alchemy. I doubt that anyone is good enough or strong enough to manage a completely worthless artist into stardom, or that anyone is incompetent enough to manage a band of superstars into the ground.

After the performers themselves, managers are probably the music-business figures most well known to the public. Much of this must be due to the success of the late Brian Epstein, who played so prominent a part in the Beatles' success. The Beatles alone might have had the cohesion and determination to overcome all obstacles and would probably have become as famous and popular as they did even without Epstein's encouragement and dedicated plugging of the band. Another example of a man who manages a band who appear to be too good to fail is Peter Grant of Led Zeppelin, but there is little doubt that Zeppelin could have got so far so smoothly without Grant's business and promotional acumen.

There are numerous and quite true stories about managers who have ripped off their acts either out of stupidity, incompetence or the lure of trying to turn a quick buck. There are also numerous cases of manager-performer personality clashes exacerbating many a band's musical problems. The relation of Allen Klein, former manager of both the Beatles and the Rolling Stones, to his artists remains a matter of much speculation (and of many lawsuits in the past), but the hassles between Klein and his most celebrated charges could hardly have lubricated the creative process. Klein is perhaps the most controversial of all the rock-and-roll managers—a man of considerable commercial perspicacity and music-business know-how who has often had stormy managerial relationships.

So these are the basic components of the music business: artist, manager, distributor, consumer. If any one of them makes a mess of his job, there's not a smooth flow—and there never is. That's the music biz.

The most common misbelief about the music business is that the distributive and manipulative machinery of the industry is so strong that any garbage that the rock panjandrums decide should be a hit will be a hit and that even the most worthless and talentless act can be made into chart toppers by the will of the men in control. This is utter nonsense. If the public are fools, they are very particular about the brand of foolishness that they will pay for. It is of course possible to get a recording contract and radio and concert exposure for almost any act, no matter how bad, with the proper combination of threat and bribery—the record business like any other industry, especially any other young industry, is susceptible to corruption and malpractice. This is unfortunate and wasteful, but when the product finally reaches the marketplace it is the individual consumer who must make the decision to accept or reject the product that he is being offered—imperfect, selective, often corrupt democracy, but still democracy when it gets to the bottom line.

No rock artist can have any measure of success without being recorded, so the record companies, by their decisions of who to record and who not to record, are important tastemakers as they ultimately control which acts will reach the public. Certain record companies, for example Atlantic Records in the late fifties and early sixties, have had a clear and vigorous artistic policy and have played a major role in shaping pop music.

Other examples are Chess Records in the fifties, which was significant in exposing black pop musicians to a large audience and, on a more modest scale, Harvest Records in the late sixties, which brought a number of the more progressive British art rockers to public attention.

The record business is a large, multibillion-dollar business—and profitable, which is why over ten thousand recordings are released every year, each one trying to get its share of the market. Most new releases get no further than a radio station wastebasket—the mortality rate among new releases is appalling, particularly in Britain, where there are fewer broadcast outlets for music—but those records which do become hits are enormous money-makers and record companies can flourish on surprisingly small hit-to-miss ratios.

Why record companies decide to sign one act and reject another is hard to say, and considering the amount of money that must be invested in a new artist —say, anywhere from twenty-five thousand to two hundred thousand dollars—the selection process is remarkably haphazard. Sometimes a new band may be similar to an established hit-maker, sometimes they may appear to fill an obvious vacuum in the market, sometimes they will be different enough to have a chance solely because of their novelty, and sometimes they may just appeal to the musical taste of record executives. Some record executives have had consistently good taste coupled with sound commercial judgment—Clive Davis at CBS, Ahmet Ertegun at Atlantic, Herb Alpert and Jerry Moss at A&M are a few examples—and their companies have profited greatly as a result.

The dramatic increase in the size of the rock market in the last ten years brought spectacular gains in revenue to the major record companies and the result was commercial gigantism, with the majors becoming increasingly powerful. There were surprisingly few attempts at consolidation, though—with the exception of the merger of Atlantic, Warner-Reprise, Elektra, and Asylum under the umbrella of Warner Communications—and the record industry remains quite fluid, with a number of small and independent labels.

A number of rock groups have attempted to exert more control over their product by forming their own labels and they have met with varying amounts of success. The first experiment in this direction was the Beatles' Apple Records, which was launched with much hoopla and many good intentions to help new performers and to give all newcomers a sympathetic listen. Apple quickly became a financial and administrative mess, and the label's most promising acts—James Taylor and Badfinger—left. When the Beatles broke up, Apple fell into disuse and wound up operations. The Rolling Stones had more modest aims with their Rolling Stones Records (hardly the most imaginative name) and have so far released only their own recordings and a few other records by friends of the band. Rolling Stones Records has not yet developed into more than a vanity label.

The most successful of the band-controlled record companies has been Swan Song, which belongs to Led Zeppelin. Swan Song discovered and signed what may be the major rock group of the mid-seventies, Bad Company, and have done an admirable job with rock veterans the Pretty Things (together in one form or another since 1964), and with singer Maggie Bell.

But after a performer gets a recording contract and makes a recording there still remains the problem of broadcast and concert exposure. Radio stations are deluged by new releases and can only play a limited number. The so-called underground stations, which are almost exclusively FM and less commercial than the major AM stations, offer more programming flexibility, but AM has the most influence over mass-market record sales, though this is changing as FM gains in importance. The job of getting records played is handled by record company promo (promotion) men who must persuade radio station programmers by various means (your guess is as good as mine, as promo men are understandably reluctant to discuss their methods) to program the records which their company has released.

Major concert appearances are equally crucial to the success of most rock acts. Of course any band that has had a number of hit records will have a little trouble being put on tour by their booking agents, but the promising new band who have yet to have a hit and who need the exposure of playing in concert may have a great deal of difficulty in finding places to play. Agents exist to marry bands who want to perform to promoters who wish to sponsor concerts, but since there are far more groups who want to perform than there are people with sufficient skill and money to promote concerts, there is a squeeze, and the agent must use his judgment, guided by artistic and/or commercial considerations, to decide which bands to sell to concert promoters. Some agents have been quite influential in shaping popular taste. Frank Barsalona in particular was instrumental in the success of a number of British groups, most notably Led Zeppelin, on the American concert market in the sixties.

The salient point about the music business is that it is much like any other business—like selling oil or dog food. The problem is that the commodity which the music business markets and distributes is an artistic creation, and every rock band, performer, and record-

116

ing, no matter how bad, is a unique and irreplaceable good, so egos and aesthetics are involved. An oil well hasn't got a personality and a rock star has, but economically they're quite similar beasts.

The rock industry is young, and perhaps too much money has been made too quickly. Like any gold rush, rock music attracts the riffraff as well as the men of quality. There are far too many jerks and crooks in the rock business, but there are also hard-working and honest people, and both groups have influenced the course of rock and roll, whether it be through faith or chicanery or skill or bad judgment. The rock industry is the infrastructure—the network that gets the music from the producer to the consumer and the money from the consumer to the producer. A little or a lot of money and music may be lost in the transaction, but the rock industry is something that we can't do without.

● ● ●

WOMEN IN ROCK

● ● ●

With the exception of Grace Slick of the Jefferson Airplane and Janis Joplin, women have not figured prominently in this version of rock history. This is not from any sexist (awful word that it is) desire to downplay or cover up the role that women have played in rock and roll. Just about half the people in the world are women, and presumably half or more than half of all the record buyers are women, yet the preponderance of rock performers have been men. Women have been a special case in rock music since the advent of the Beatles and so deserve special consideration for their place in rock and roll since 1964.

In the early rock years there were a number of

prominent women rock performers: Sylvia of Mickey and Sylvia, LaVern Baker, the Teddy Bears, Brenda Lee, Rosie and the Originals, The Shirelles, Carla Thomas, and others. The coming of the Beatles and the resultant dominance of self-contained rock groups effectively put an end to mainstream female participation in rock and roll, as there were few women bassists, guitar players, and drummers around—partially because these were not the traditionally feminine instruments and it was thought, with some reason, that a rock group with flute, piano, and harp would have limited commercial appeal. The few women performers who could be found on the charts continued to perform in the old format of solo artist backed up by orchestra: Marianne Faithfull, Cilla Black, and Sandi Shaw, who all had chart success in the days of the British invasion, conformed to this setup.

From 1964 on women rock performers were cast in the archaic mold, first for the purely technical reason that there were few women skilled in the playing of the new rock group instruments and second because the revitalized rock produced by the Beatles, the Stones, and their contemporaries was incompatible with accepted social canons of feminine behavior. It was quite all right for the boys to play and sing musical intimations of teen-age mattress dancing, but it just wouldn't do to have girls mouthing such filth, so as rock became raunchier and more vigorous women were relegated to the backwaters of the scene.

⌐It must also be noted that the most fanatic early supporters of the new rock groups tended to be mostly young girls who were perhaps more interested in having a fantasy boyfriend figure on stage than in furthering the cause of women's right to aesthetic expression through rock music.

The San Francisco bands, who were generally so completely out in left field—so, like, Counter-cultural, man—that they probably had no idea when they were flouting social rules, were the first rock groups to bring women back into the creative mainstream of rock and roll, as the success of both Grace Slick and Janis Joplin attests. Grace Slick's popularity was always limited by the eccentric and esoteric style of Jefferson Airplane—a style which she helped forge—but Joplin became a national pop idol, and had she not died so early in her career, she might have become one of rock and roll's dominant performers. But few other women followed in the Joplin/Slick mold and rose to prominence as vocalists with rock groups.

It seemed that the most socially acceptable way for women to make their mark as pop-music figures in the sixties was as sensitive singer-songwriter types who listlessly strummed guitars or stroked piano keys and wrote hit songs for themselves and others. Joni Mitchell is perhaps the most outstanding example of this. She has written and recorded some first-rate music but she remains more celebrated as a songwriter than as a performer.

The major break into rock stardom by a woman in recent years was made by Carol King, who has been in the music business since the late fifties when she was a phenomenally successful songwriter in collaboration with Gerry Goffin. She embarked on a solo career as a performer in the late sixties and reached something slightly more rarified than superstardom with her 1972 album, *Tapestry,* which, with over ten million copies sold, is perhaps the biggest selling rock album ever. Although King failed to follow *Tapestry* with any equally strong recordings, her presence on the music scene remained strong. Still, like Joni Mitchell and other women songwriters, her softer, more musical style of pop was hardly at the center of a music scene dominated by Heavy Rock.

The first all-woman rock band to be in the musical center of things was Fanny, a quartet formed in 1970 who played competent and on occasion interesting hard rock. Fanny were not really very good—they could hardly compare to Led Zep or the Faces—but they proved that women could be tough, perform some pretty nasty songs, and play electric guitars without turning into freaked-out harridans. Other female rock groups, including Isis, a heavily promoted New York outfit, appeared in the wake of Fanny's acceptance if not success, but the first authentic woman hard-rock star was an expatriated American who first scored heavily with English audiences.

Suzi Quatro came from a musical Detroit family— her brother Michael is a rock musician and her sister Patti plays with Fanny. After playing in a number of local bands with limited success, she went to Britain under the tutelage of Mickie Most, one of rock's most successful entrepreneurs. Quatro has had a number of hit records in Britain, with songs written for her by Mike Chapman and Nicky Chinn, and has become a major figure on the British music scene, but she has been unable to achieve any comparable success in the United States. Suzi is unquestionably a hard rocker, sings suggestive songs, plays bass guitar, and runs around in gold lamé or black-leather jump suits—a tough-chick stage image and an energetic and talented performer. She is possibly the only contemporary woman rock performer who can compete with the currently dominant rock stars on their own, essentially masculine, terms. While Quatro lacks the virtuoso talent of a Jimmy Page, she certainly has ample musical and personal appeal to become an established rock star.

The question must be: Will society in general and the rock audience in particular allow women to be rock-and-roll stars? I think not, at least not for a while. The qualities of raunchiness, outrage, and naked physical energy which are the sine qua nons of rock stardom remain inconsistent with accepted standards of women's behavior and so must militate against many women seeking artistic expression as rock performers. Women will probably continue to be more significant in rock and roll as composers and recording artists rather than as concert performers. Much of the audience support for rock acts is initially fired by the enthusiasm of the youngest and most excitable fans, who are usually girls, and it seems likely that the female weenies will continue to give most of their support to male performers. Further, the traditions of the last decade which have been slanted against women rock performers will continue to serve as a brake on women becoming rock performers.

Of course some women will always figure in rock and roll as performers and there will be new Joplins and Quatros. Currently there is a strong demand for women performers as indicated by the record sales of performers like Kiki Dee, Carly Simon, Minnie Ripperton, and Linda Ronstadt. But it will be a long while before women get an equal piece of the rock-and-roll action.

● ● ●
ROCK AND ROLL TECHNOLOGY
● ● ●

Aesthetics are conditioned by the technology of artistic expression at any given time. Just as tempera expressed and circumscribed medieval visual art, so oil paint was required by and helped to define early modern visual standards. Rock and roll has always been a high technology art dependent not on the work of a few skilled craftsmen for its tools—as, let us say, classical music depends on a supply of violin-making craftsmen—but instead on manufacturers, laborers, and bureaucrats. Rock has long used electric instruments which require electric amplification and has always depended on recordings as its principal medium. So rock is to an extent a child of the factory workers who operate record-pressing machines and who work on assembly lines in guitar factories; a creation of the transcontinental power grid and the men who must dig ceaselessly for Con Ed. Rock may sound primitive, but like universities and frozen shrimp chow mein it is a product of highly civilized societies.

The relation between any art and its technology is subtle and complex. Ever more powerful amplifiers were needed to produce the sound levels of heavy rock, but heavy rock would not have been possible without the big amps. The music has always been very conscious of technology because technology often gives the competitive edge to those who know how to use it. New technology always has at least a novelty value.

One of the most unpleasant sounds a guitar is capable of producing is made with the aid of a device called a fuzz box, which makes a guitar sound as though it were being played through the back end of an elephant. The fuzz box sound made its debut on a great early British rock single, the Rolling Stones' *Satisfaction,* and in no time at all its electric borborygmy was ubiquitous. The fuzz box mercifully faded away after not too long—though it may still be heard among a few relentless *nostalgie de la boue* bands—but its popularity, though short-lived, inspired a number of other devices such as treble boosters, sustain units, and wah-wah pedals, which could alter the sound of an electric guitar. Rock guitarists are always looking for just the right touch of sonic weirdness, and the fuzz box and successor apparatuses have whetted their appetites for more sound-altering gadgets.

But the true hyper-zaarged-out electronic-sound addicts are usually art rockers and keyboard players and most especially Art Rock keyboard players.

For technical and psychological reasons keyboard players have been the most willing victims of electrosonic devices, both good and bad. For years organists and pianists have played supporting roles in the rock musician hierarchy, devotedly pounding away at grand pianos and Hammond organs while their mobile guitar-wielding fellow performers dashed wildly about the stage garnering the largest shares of audience oohs and aahs. True, a few virtuoso players like Keith Emerson, Brian Auger and Nicky Hopkins attracted some attention, but rock and roll remained a guitar player's game until . . .

Until was supplied by Doctor Robert Moog (rhymes with *Vogue*), an electronics engineer from New York, who designed and built the Moog Synthesizer, an awesome bundle of wires, resistors, capacitors, and other bits that were capable of generating an almost unlimited number of sounds both euphonious and markedly unpleasant. The Moog was a keyboard instrument and, although its size and complexity precluded any mad running about with it, the stunning and shocking sounds which the Moog and other synthesizers which followed produced drew attention to keyboardists as never before. The turn to synthesizers was also a result of the influence on Art Rock bands of "serious" modern composers like Stockhausen who used other than traditional instrumental sounds in their music.

The first of the flashy synthesizer-playing keyboardists was Keith Emerson, whose band—Emerson, Lake, and Palmer—combined a dazzling stage show with an extremely well played farrago of classical, modern, and pop music. Rick Wakeman, first in the British rock band Yes and then as a solo artist, shared top honors with Emerson as the leading gaudy techno-keyboardists. By 1974 synthesizers had proliferated through the rock world so thoroughly that scarcely a pop performer failed to make use of one at some stage. Synthesizers will of course never replace conventional instruments, but they are the most versatile and potentially exciting instruments to appear for a long while, and now, almost exclusively because of their use by so many rock musicians, they have become accepted and often-used musical instruments rather than just novelty noise-making devices.

The environment of the concert hall and the recording studio make rock particularly sensitive to technology for both economic and aesthetic reasons. Because rock and roll relied from the start on amplified instruments—the electric guitar (an inheritance from the blues and country traditions) principally—rock-and-roll performers were able to go beyond the boundaries of audience size imposed by acoustic instruments and play to increasingly larger numbers of people. The equation was simple: better equipment made it possible to play to larger crowds, larger crowds meant more money. There was an impetus to develop bigger and better speakers and amplifiers for on-stage use, and these more powerful amplifiers made new sounds possible: Led Zeppelin couldn't have existed in 1965.

Records are the principal medium for the presentation of pop-rock music, and the relentless technicality of the recording studio forced rock and rollers to be attuned to the hardware—and much of it was quite sophisticated even in the antediluvian days of 1964—of their trade. The recording studio, where so much of the rock sound was shaped, was the aesthetic-technical skirmish line of the art. One of rock and roll's greatest leaps forward—apologies to Chairman Mao—was the realization that recordings could be an independent means of artistic expression, not just a copy of the performer's in-concert sound. The studio became in effect yet another instrument, and the men who controlled the recording process—the recording engineers and the producer—became quasi-members of the band.

A record producer is the mediator between a performer and the technology of recording, the one who directs the recording session and helps the performer to create his music on record. As recording techniques developed, the role of the producer changed. In the fifties, when recording was a relatively simple process —few tricks aside from double tracking and fiddling with the tone controls were possible—the producer was often a combination of songwriter-entrepreneur and artistic boss, as the famous team of Jerry Leiber and Mike Stoller were. The producer found or wrote a song, found a performer, and put together what he thought should be a hit. But as tape recorders, sound-mixing boards, and studio technology and microphones and studio technology in general developed and opened new possibilities for the manipulation of sound on tape, the record producer became more involved in the recording process and less involved with the externals.

Once again it was the Beatles who were in the

vanguard of change. As the Beatles rose to ever more vertiginous heights, so did all those associated with them, and George Martin, their producer, became quite celebrated as an important factor in the creation of the Beatles' sound with his arrangements and feel for the group's music. The Beatles' 1966 album, *Revolver*, and 1967 single, *Strawberry Fields*, were, I think, the first indications of the complexity and richness of thoughtfully recorded rock and roll, but it was *Sgt. Pepper's Lonely Hearts Club Band*, with its brilliant engineering by Geoff Emerick, which marked the major breakthrough to a new, more mature and artistically more independent way of recording rock and roll. Contemporaneously, but on a less exalted level, Cream were making major advances in the studio under the guidance of their producer, Felix Pappalardi.

Everyone became quite producer-crazy and producers like George Martin, Eddie Kramer, Glyn Johns, Jimmy Miller, and others became stars in their own right. While certain earlier producers like Bob Johnston, who produced Bob Dylan and Simon and Garfunkel, had been well known, it was only after *Sgt. Pepper* that the record-buying public had any special awareness of producers as important creative personalities.

Whether great producers help artists to make great records or great artists help producers to make great records is problematical, as, in a way, a great song is a rather independent creature which often comes to the fore regardless of the ineptitude of or the skill of the artist or the producer. At any rate, the artist/producer relationship is symbiotic: they both need each other, though it is difficult to tell who gains most from the transaction. What is certain is that the new importance of the producer and public awareness of his part is

indicative of both the growing complexity and resultant division of labor in the rock world and the need of
rock and roll and indeed of all popular mass arts to fuel
the public with ever more stars and celebrities.

NEW THRILLS FOR
THE JADED GENERATION
1972-1975

The exciting and prodigious pluralism of the late sixties and early seventies was regrettably short-lived, as social and economic forces brought on a hardening of the rock-and-roll arteries. As rock succeeded in entrenching itself into society and becoming a significant part of the quotidian life of eight-year-old school children and thirty-five-year-old housewives, it came to be more stratified and more "well-targeted" in marketing terms. As the teen-agers who had jived to Buddy Holly in the fifties reached the threshold of middle age and constituted the upper chronological limit of the rock audience, the demographic base broadened at the bottom as the youngest generation of fans—the eight- to twelve-year-olds who were raised in a world where rock was an aural commonplace and had missed the Heroic Age of 1964—came into the market.

It is a truism that the very young are less discriminating than more mature consumers, not that the more mature are all that discriminating. The realization that there was a mass of young, pliable, and easily manipulated consumers who either had money to spend or could influence the spending of money ("If you don't buy me the latest Lance and the Jamjars album, I'll hold my breath til I turn purple") meant an inevitable decline in the quality of music that would be offered to these consumers, since all popular and commercialized art not only tends to, but strives for, the lowest common denominator. These microboppers wanted different things from music than their older fellow rock-and-roll fans, who wanted songs that were about dope or made them feel weird in the genitals or had some musical validity. These boppers didn't know from sex, drugs, revolution, or music: they just wanted someone pretty to look at who sang about puppy love. On the other hand, older rock fans are rather better educated musically than the rock fans of, say, 1967 and so demand generally higher standards of musicianship.

All through the age spectrum of rock fans, popular taste—unless one happened to be either a Japanese businessman or a Bahreini sheikh—was being colored by the worsening national and international economy and by the resultant monetary squeeze. So, for a while, fewer consumer dollars, or at least more carefully spent dollars, were chasing an increasing number of acts. This meant that pop performers had to be either more sensitive to public taste or more outrageous and more different than ever before in order to attract enough support to survive. Consequently there was a redistribution of wealth and patronage in the rock world, and as the superstar cult continued to grow, the major performers began making more money than ever before—it was increasingly common for the top rock acts to earn about one hundred thousand dollars a performance. So as the room at the top of the rock heap gets smaller and the scramble for a share of the audience becomes more intense, performers must fight for their place either by pandering to the least discriminating members of the audience or by being even more outré or weird or by becoming more specialized and offering a more intense distillation of their style. As a result, the world of rock and roll has become more stratified and compartmentalized in recent years, and much of the healthy musical cross-fertilization of the preceding half-decade has slowed or ceased.

A major innovation was the introduction of teen and pre-teen rock stars. As the established rock performers aged—by 1972 the Beatles were all in their thirties—they grew more distant from the newly important microbopper audience. The first group to make the chronological breakthrough was the Jackson Five, a black family rock act fronted by singer Michael Jackson, who was ten at the time of the band's first hit single in 1970. The J5 purveyed popped-up soul music and were quickly followed into the charts by the Osmond Brothers, a tabernacle of Mormons who had kicked around show business for years and bore an uncanny musical resemblance to the Jackson Five. Apart from the obvious racial difference, the major dissimilarity between the two groups was that the J5 were talented while the Osmonds were precociously innocuous. It seemed that the Osmonds' success was due to their being a white, homogenized Jackson Five. Both bands were quite successful, but the Osmonds, and particularly little brother Donny, became transatlantic stars. In an effort to capitalize on the success of both the J5 and the Osmonds, a television series about a family rock group, the Partridge Family, was aired in the United States. In conjunction with the series the Partridge Family released a number of singles which were mostly the work of side men, but producer Wes Farrel decided that the leader of the Partridges, David Cassidy, could sing, and so Cassidy with his youthful, clean-cut looks and tenuous musical talents was launched as another microbopper heart throb.

For some reason the pre-teen market in Britain, although much smaller than that in the United States, was more buoyant, and aside from receiving American teeny stars with enthusiasm, the British audience fanatically supported a number of home-grown heroes including groups and performers like Slade, the Sweet, Mud, and the Bay City Rollers. Indeed the Bay City Rollers, a quintet of young Scots, were accorded hysterical receptions that rivaled the Beatlemania of the early sixties. It was good to see the teenies displaying such enthusiasm for their favorites at a time when the hippest attitude was to be jaded and blasé, but their enthusiasm may not serve to make the rock scene as exciting as it once was when audiences tended to be more passionately and intelligently partisan. Beatlemania was beneficial to the pop-music scene because the enthusiastic response which the Beatles elicited from their early fans alerted the public to the Beatles' talent and had a sort of spillover effect, since the Beatles were talented enough to justify the fan hysteria which they generated. Such is hardly the case with the Bay City Rollers, whose musical talent is at best exiguous. Fans of the Rollers and other bands who are teeny fave raves often regard the music as secondary and support their favorite bands because they are "nice"—pretty to look at and the sort of boyfriend that every girl would hope to have. Most of the very young record buyers are girls and this of course tilts the market in favor of good-looking and musically innocuous bands.

One of rock's more bizarre personalities was Vince Furnier, who, under the name of Alice Cooper, led his eponymous band from being androgynous protégés of the Los Angeles cult group the Mothers of Invention to Anglo-American stardom on the basis of a few catchy rock songs and a stage show of unparalleled bad taste and morbidity which featured gallows, electric chairs, boa constrictors, and chicken strangling. Pretty high-powered stuff, much condemned as being damaging to teen and pre-teen morals and sensibilities, but brains that thrive naturally on such garbage can hardly be further damaged. Performing excesses aside, Cooper could turn out some decent rock and roll.

Alice was the first of a crop of sexually ambiguous rockers and razzle-dazzle glitter stars who sought attention through an image of unmitigated chrome-plated maladjustment. The leading figures of the style were two Englishmen, Marc Bolan with his group, T. Rex, and David Bowie. Bolan was an inveterate trendy, being at various times a snazzy young mod, a model, a mystic folk-rocker poet, and a psychedelic type, before becoming an extravagantly and in a freaked-out way elegantly dressed hard rocker who was pretty to look at for the girls and played tough music for the boys. Bolan had a huge following in Britain, but failed to make it big in the United States. David Bowie, whose professional path had crossed Bolan's on occasion, was a different case.

Bowie is one of the most unusual and excessive figures in pop-music history. He was the first visually bisexual rock star; he had his hair dyed orange, wore amazing make-up, and dressed like a cross between Esther Williams and Flash Gordon. Bowie is a memorable figure solely by virtue of his flamboyant stage performance and startling—I didn't say attractive because it's actually quite repulsive—visual image, but he has also written and performed some outstanding rock songs including his early hit "Space Odditty," which was one of the first pop tunes about space exploration. A number of less talented performers picked up the epicene glam glitter of Bolan and Bowie, but none of them have had the talent to make much of an impact. Bowie and Bolan were influential among rock groups as the leaders of a trend toward more sophisticated and unusual rock costuming after the rather low-key style of dress (jeans, workshirts, and army surplus gear) in the late sixties.

Heavy Rock continued unabated as a dominant trend in rock and roll and the position of the world's most popular rock group was contested by Led Zeppelin and Deep Purple, a band who scored their first hit in 1969 and after personnel and musical changes emerged as sophisticated ultra-heavies.

Lead by the saturnine if not positively satanic Ritchie Blackmore, a guitarist of great strength and lyricism, Deep Purple have had a succession of successful singles and albums. Although they are unquestionably ultra-heavies—tagged as the world's loudest rock group by the Guinness Book of World Records—Purple are a band of surprisingly refined sensibilities that put them streets ahead of the other Heavy Rock groups. They eventually broke up due to differences between Blackmore and keyboard player Jon Lord.

Led Zeppelin's following and talent appear to increase yearly, and for me and many others they are the ultimate rock-and-roll band: direct and powerful almost to the point of brutality, yet informed by a graceful subtlety that is unique to rock and roll.

The Beatles as individuals and the Rolling Stones have by now become the elder statesmen of rock and roll. The Stones have failed to equal the musical achievements of their earlier albums like *Let It Bleed,* but their concerts and recordings continue to appeal to a widening audience and they are the only rock group who have become cult figures to all who profess to be "with it" members of modern society. Individually the Beatles remain a major force in pop music, though their memory as a group may be fading. Paul McCartney, with inexhaustible charm and melodic good sense, formed a group, Wings, to support him and recorded *Band on the Run,* which many consider to be the best rock album of 1974. George Harrison has been cloaked in a fog of Oriental mysticism and his recent recorded work has made little impact. John Lennon continues sporadically to produce listenable and often quite excellent rock and roll, but his occasional performances in the role of the twentieth century's leading pseudointellectual often make him a bit hard to take. Surprisingly, because he was considered the musical dud of the group, Ringo Starr has become a major record seller, and his *Ringo* album was thoroughly enjoyable and interesting.

The only relatively new performer to rise to the stature of longer established rock stars in recent years has been Elton John, an extraordinary English pianist-vocalist, who, in collaboration with lyricist Bernie Taupin, has written and recorded a large number of compelling and original rock songs. The extravagance of John's stage show, his garish clothing, oversized glasses, and eccentric life-style have undoubtedly helped him reach a wide audience, but the sensitivity, quality, and authentic rock-and-roll gut feeling of his writing and performing have established him as one of rock and roll's major talents.

And so the rock scene a decade after the Beatles rocketed into prominence. The excitement has flickered and faded a bit, but still remains. We are all more jaded: there has been too much cultural shock and trauma in the last ten years. Our sensibilities are less sharp than they once were. The Beatles raised cries of outrage because their hair was, say, an inch or two longer than the norm and because the lapels on their suits (suits!) were different from what the canons of fashion allowed. Today a rock group would have to have a hermaphroditic guitar player who copulated with a rhinoceros on stage to cause more than a whisper of protest. Only the ability of the music to affect us has remained constant over the years. We progress and our music progresses with us—the destination remains uncertain.

NEAR THE END OF
THE TRAIL:
THE LEVI-ING OF AMERICA

In 1976 rock and roll occupied a more prominent place in our society than ever before, but it was rock and roll as a culture, or rather the cultural trappings, which came in the train of rock and roll. The storm troopers of the rock audience were still teen-agers and young adults, and the best, most vigorous, and authentic rock music was still aimed at them and supported by them. Of course the teenies scream and faint because of the warblings and gyrations of their latest heart throbs—perhaps they will learn better—and the superficial aspects of rock and roll can be found almost everywhere in the music world: Bar Mitzvah bands and Lawrence Welk alike have been influenced by rock and roll.

Rock and roll was and is the great music of our times, and although it is now appealing to both an older and a younger audience than ever before, it may finally have reached its demographic limits. Rock and roll remains the music of the young. It has all the pretenses, excesses, and poses that only the young can fall for, which is one reason why being young is such a wonderful thing. Rock may develop into an art form which is capable of expressing the loftiest and most refined sentiments—it has not yet done so. After twenty years rock and roll is a music of unprecedented power and intensity, but not of contemplation and nobility. It is a music which celebrates rather than explains life, and so it remains a music of youth and adolescence rather than maturity.

But the cultural spillover effects of rock and roll have been so profound that it is difficult not to exaggerate the artistic importance of the music. Rock has been the great force of social liberation of the last decade—a music and a life-style of libertarianism and individuality. The overwhelming commercial and aesthetic victory of rock as popular music promoted and sanctioned the eccentricity and studied bohemianism with which rock performers called attention to themselves and their music. Rock and roll may be viewed negatively as the triumph of tastelessness over taste, of gratuitous nonconformism over shared patterns of behavior, but rock and roll is an ongoing and institutionalized cultural side show, an endorsement of the individual personality rather than the glib blandness of modern corporate existence.

However, the rapidity with which blue jeans, bright clothing, free sex and dope-smoking spread from the rock-and-roll vanguard throughout society has little to do with the small man standing up against big government and the big corporations and much to do with the pathetic chasing after youth which the older members of our society indulge in. We have become a youth-oriented society for reasons of commerce and not of philosophy. Youth buy more and know less. What could be more ideal for the men who make Brand X and Brand Y than a country full of youths who buy, buy, buy, never become bored with novelty, and never question. Everyone had to be made young. Fifty-year-old East Side women had to be convinced that they should wear studded Levis and their fifty-year-old executive husbands had to be convinced to grow their sideburns long and wear Apache scarves on the weekend. Everyone had to be young and with it and what could be more young and with it than rock and roll? Everyone had to rock and roll. And before long, rock and roll became just the greatest thing ever; the path to youth, beauty, money, fame, forever and ever. But that's the sort of thing that kids are meant to fall for, and instead the dream—and we know it's a dream—is being stolen by over-the-hill socialites and university professors who take it all seriously. Christ, they might even convince us that they're right.

That's what began to happen as rock and roll—not the music but the way that we listen and react to it—changed from a thing of savage and evanescent beauty to something to agonize over and analyze and philosophize about, and it all becomes terribly serious and academic and not as much fun as it was and should be.

The teenies and the microboppers may be the most fortunate, for although the music they listen to may be garbage, they just listen for the kick they get from it. We have to cherish that kick and keep it from slipping away. Rock and roll is so important, so much a part of who we are and how we feel, that we must think about it, read about it, even—God help us—write about it, but at the same time we can't allow ourselves to forget the thrill of it all. The sheer physical sensation of Deep Purple at one hundred and ten decibels or the charming melodic grace of a McCartney tune.

Rock and roll has no time for futurism or nostalgia: it flourishes in and celebrates only the timelessness of the present. Rock and roll is a present that we have given ourselves.

INDEX

Agents, 116
Allman, Duane, 94
Allman Brothers Band, 94, 95
"All You Need Is Love" (Beatles), 36
Alpert, Herb, 114
Altamont Festival, 83–84, 90
A & M Records, 114
Amboy Dukes, 94
American Bandstand, 106
Anderson, Ian, 100–1
Animals, 38, 48, 58, 88
Apple Records, 115
Are You Experienced? (Hendrix), 88
Art Rock, 96, 98, 108; keyboard players, 123–24
Asylum Records, 115
Atlantic Records, 113, 114, 115
Auger, Brian, 123
Avalon Ballroom, 72

Bad Company, 115
Badfinger, 115

Baez, Joan, 65
Bailey, David, 49
Baker, Ginger, 57, 87, 95
Baker, La Vern, 118
Ballard, Hank *see* Hank Ballard and the Midnighters
Band on the Run (Wings), 137
Band, The, 98
Barsalona, Frank, 116
Bay City Rollers, 110, 134
Beach Boys, 67–70; "409," 70; "Little Deuce Coupe," 70; "Surfer Girl," 68; "Surfin' Safari," 68; "Surfin' USA," 68
Beatlemania, 134
Beatles, 16, 32–38, 40, 43, 44, 45, 46, 53, 54, 55, 57, 61, 67, 89, 90, 97, 101, 112, 117, 118, 137, 138; "All You Need Is Love," 36; Apple Records, 115; breakup, 87, 98; compared to Stones, 46–47, 48, 49; "For the Benefit of Mr. Kite," 86; influence of West Coast sound on, 85–87; "I Want

to Hold Your Hand," 34; "Love Me Do," 34; "Please, Please Me," 34; production of, 125–26; *Revolver,* 86, 126; *Rubber Soul,* 86; *Sergeant Pepper,* 85–86, 126; "She Loves You," 34; as stars, 107; Stones song written by, 48; "Strawberry Fields," 126; "Til There Was You," 36

Beau Brummels, 38

Bedford, Duke of, 36

Beck, Jeff, 56. *See also* Jeff Beck Group

Beefeaters *see* Byrds

Beggars Banquet (Stones), 99

Belafonte, Harry, 62

Bell, Maggie, 115

Berry, Chuck, 22–23, 48

Big Brother and the Holding Company, 71, 89

Bill Haley and the Comets, 17–18, 106; "Rock Around the Clock," 17; "Shake, Rattle, and Roll," 17. *See also* Haley, Bill

Black, Cilla, 118

Blackboard Jungle, 18

Blackmore, Ritchie, 92, 136

Black Sabbath, 93–94, 101

Blind Faith, 95–96

Bloodrock: "DOA," 94

Blood, Sweat and Tears, 98

Bolan, Marc, 135, 136

Bonham, John, 92

Bowie, David, 135–36; "Space Oddity," 136

"Bridge Over Troubled Waters" (Simon), 97

Brown, Pete, 57

Bruce, Jack, 57, 87

Buffalo Springfield, 94

Byrds, 66–67, 94

California, 68–70, 71–75. *See also* Altamont Festival *and* West Coast scene

Calypso, 4

Cardin, Pierre, 41

Cassidy, David, 134

CBS Records, 114

Chandler, Chas, 88

Chapman, Mike, 120

Checker, Chubby, 36

Chess Records, 114

Chicago (group), 98

Chinn, Nicky, 120

Chords: "Sh-Boom," 16–17

Christie, Lew: "Two Faces Have I," 31

Clapton, Eric, 56, 57, 87, 92, 95, 109. *See also* Cream *and* Yardbirds

Cochrane, Eddie, 23

Cocker, Joe, 99

Colosseum, 99

Concerts, 116

Cooper, Alice *see* Furnier, Vince

Counter-culture, 76–78, 90

Country-and-western music, 18–19

Courrèges, André, 41

Coward, Noel, 36

Cream, 56–58, 90, 92; *Disraeli Gears,* 85, 87–88; *Fresh Cream,* 57; "Sunshine of Your Love," 88; "Toad," 57; *Wheels of Fire,* 91

Creedance Clearwater Revival, 94–95, 101; "Susie Q," 95

Crew Cuts: "Sh-Boom," 17

Crosby, Stills, Nash and Young, 78, 94

Daltrey, Roger, 53

Dantalian's Chariot, 84

Dave Dee Dozy Beeky Mick and Tich, 53

Davis, Clive, 114

Dee, Kiki, 121

Deep Purple, 108, 136

Delaney and Bonnie, 99

Dion and the Belmonts, 106

Disraeli Gears (Cream), 85, 87–88

"DOA" (Bloodrock), 94

Dolly birds, 42

Donegan, Lonnie: "Rock Island Line," 33

Donovan *see* Leitch, Donovan

Doors, 99

Downer Rock, 90, 93–94, 98

Dylan, Bob, 65–67, 97, 98, 126

"Earth Angel," 17

Ed Sullivan Show, 3

Electric Prunes, 94
Elektra Records, 115
Emerick, Geoff, 126
Emerson, Keith, 123, 124
Emerson, Lake, and Palmer, 124
EMI, 34
Entwhistle, John, 53
Epstein, Brian, 34, 40, 112
Eric Burdon and the New Animals, 84
Ertegun, Ahmet, 114
Everly Brothers, 3, 23

Fabian, 24, 106
Faces, 98–99
Fairport Convention, 96
Faithfull, Marianne, 118
Fanny, 120
Farrel, Wes, 134
Fascist Rock, 91
Fashion, 41–46
Fillmore, 72
Films, 18–19, 35, 68–69
Fleetwood Mac, 99
Flock, 101
Flying Burrito Brothers, 99
Fogerty, John, 95
Folk music, 32, 62–64, 110
Fontana, Wayne, 53
"For the Benefit of Mister Kite" (Beatles), 86
"For Your Love" (Yardbirds), 56
Fourmost, 38
"409" (Beach Boys), 70
Free, 99
Freeman, Robert, 35
Fresh Cream (Cream), 57–58
Furnier, Vince (Alice Cooper), 135
Fury, Billy, 33
Fuzz box, 122–23

Garfunkel, Art, 97
Generation gap, 77
Gerry and the Pacemakers, 48
"Get Off of My Cloud" (Stones), 86
Gidget, 69
"Gimme Some Lovin'" (Spencer Davis Group), 56
Goffin, Gerry, 119
"Goodnight, Irene, Goodnight," 17

"Good Times, Bad Times" (Led Zeppelin), 92
Gore, Leslie: "It's My Party," 31
Graham, Bill, 72
Graham Bond Organization, 48, 57
Grand Funk Railroad, 93, 94
Grant, Peter, 112
Grateful Dead, 71
Green, Peter, 99
"Green Manalishi, The" (Fleetwood Mac), 99
Groupies, 109
Guinness Book of World Records, 136

Haley, Bill, 22
Hamilton, Richard, 39
Hank Ballard and the Midnighters: "Sexy Ways," 19; "Work with Me, Annie," 19
Harrison, George, 37, 98, 137. *See also* Beatles
Harvest Records, 114
Hawkins, Dale, 95
"Heat Wave" (Martha and the Vandellas), 31
Heavy Rock, 90, 91–93, 94, 95, 96, 98, 100, 108, 120, 122, 136
Helms, Chet, 72
Hendrix, Jimi, 88–90, 92; *Are You Experienced?* 88; "Purple Haze," 88. *See also* Jimi Hendrix Experience
Herman's Hermits, 53
High Numbers *see* Who, The
Hippies, 73–76
Hockney, David, 41
Hollies, 58, 94
Holly, Buddy, 23, 106–7, 131
Hopkins, Nicky, 123
Howling Wolf, 47
Hullabaloos, 73
Humble Pie, 98

"I'm a Man" (Yardbirds), 56
Iron Butterfly, 99
Isis, 120
"It's My Party" (Leslie Gore), 31
"I Wanna Be Your Man" (Stones), 48

"I Want to Hold Your Hand" (Beatles), 34

Jackson, Michael, 133
Jackson Five, 133
Jagger, Mick, 49–50, 92, 107. See also Rolling Stones
"Jailhouse Rock" (Presley), 22
Jan and Dean: "Surf City," 68
Jeff Beck Group, 92. See also Beck, Jeff
Jefferson Airplane, 71, 78, 83, 117, 119
Jesus Christ Superstar, 100
Jethro Tull, 100–1
Jimi Hendrix Experience, 97. See also Hendrix, Jimi
John, Elton, 108, 109, 137–38
Johns, Glyn, 126
Johnston, Bob, 126
Jones, Brian, 50
Jones, John Paul, 92
Joplin, Janis, 89–90, 117, 119

Kent State University, 93
King, Carol, 119–20; Tapestry, 119
King Crimson, 99
Kingston Trio, 62–63, 65; "Tom Dooley," 63
Kinks, 43, 58
Klein, Allen, 112
Knight, Terry, 93
Korner, Alexis, 47, 55
Kramer, Eddie, 126

Led Zeppelin, 91–93, 108, 112, 116, 120, 124, 136; "Good Times, Bad Times," 92; Led Zeppelin, 92; Swan Song Records, 115; "Stairway to Heaven," 93
Lee, Brenda, 118
Leiber, Jerry, 125
Leiber and Stoller, 21–22
Leitch, Donovan, 56
Lennon, John, 37, 98, 137. See also Beatles
Let It Bleed (Stones), 99, 137
Lewis, Jerry Lee, 23
Light shows, 72
"Little Deuce Coupe" (Beach Boys), 70

"Living Doll" (Cliff Richard), 34
London, Laurie, 33
Lord, John, 136
Love, 99
"Love Me Do" (Beatles), 34
LSD, 72
Lulu, 53

Managers, 111–12
Manne, Manfred, 57
Martha and the Vandellas: "Heat Wave," 31
Martin, George, 34, 126
Mass art, 12–15, 20
Mayall, John, 48, 54, 99
McCartney, Paul, 8, 37, 98, 107, 137. See also Beatles
MC5, 94
McGuinn, Jim, 67
Meek, Joe, 33
Mickey and Sylvia, 118
Microboppers, 132–34
Miller, Jimmy, 126
Mills Brothers, 36
"Mr. Tambourine Man" (Dylan), 67; Byrds' recording, 67
Mitchell, Joni, 119
Moby Grape, 71
Mod movement, 43
Monterey Pop Festival, 89
Moody Blues, 100
Moog, Robert, 123
Moog Synthesizer, 123–24
Moon, Keith, 53, 92
Moss, Jerry, 114
Most, Mickie, 56, 120
Mothers of Invention, 135
Mud, 134
"My Generation" (Who), 54

Nazz, 99
Newport Folk Festival, 66
New York, 78
Nice, 96

Osmond, Donny, 133
Osmond Brothers, 133
"Over Under Sideways Down" (Yardbirds), 56

Page, Jimmy, 56, 92, 120
Pappalardi, Felix, 126
Partridge Family, 134
Peter, Paul and Mary, 62, 65
Phonographs, 7
Pink Floyd, 96
Plant, Robert, 92
"Please, Please Me" (Beatles), 34
"Poison Ivy," 22
Pop artists, 39
Pop music, 10–16, 97
Porter, Cole, 19
Presley, Elvis, 22, 23, 105–6, 107
Pretty Things, 115
Privilege (film), 35
Procol Harum, 96
"Purple Haze" (Hendrix), 88

Quant, Mary, 41
Quatro, Suzi, 120
Quickly, Tommy, 53
Quicksilver Messenger Service, 71

Race records, 16
Radio, 9–10, 115–16
Radziwill, Lee, 36
Ray, Johnny, 35
Rebel Without a Cause, 18
Record business, 113–16
Record producers, 125–27
Records, 7–10, 125–27
Revolver (Beatles), 86, 126
Rhythm-and-blues, 16–17, 18, 19
Rice, Tim, 100
Richard, Cliff, 33–34; "Living
  Doll," 34
Richard, Keith, 50. *See also* Roll-
  ing Stones
Ringo (Ringo Starr), 137
Ripperton, Minnie, 121
Rivingtons: "Surfer Bird," 31
Rock and roll, 16–24
"Rock and Roll Music" (Berry), 22
"Rock Around the Clock" (Bill Ha-
  ley), 17, 18
"Rock Island Line" (Lonnie Done-
  gan), 33
Rolling Stones, 38, 40, 46–51, 53,
  54, 55, 57, 90, 100, 112, 118; at
  Altamont, 83–84; *Beggars Ban-
  quet,* 99; compared to Beatles,
46–47, 48, 49; "Get Off of My
  Cloud," 86; influence of West
  Coast sound on, 85, 87; "I
  Wanna Be Your Man," 48; *Let It
  Bleed,* 99, 137; Rolling Stones
  Records, 115; "Satisfaction,"
  122; as stars, 107; *Sticky Fingers,*
  99; *Their Satanic Majesties Re-
  quest,* 85, 87, 99
Rolling Stones Records, 115
Ronstadt, Linda, 121
Rosie and the Originals, 118
Rubber Soul (Beatles), 86
Rydell, Bobby, 24

San Francisco Sound, 71–75
Santana, 78
Sassoon, Vidal, 41
"Satisfaction" (Stones), 122
Screaming Lord Sutch, 41
Searchers, 48
Seeger, Pete, 64
*Sgt. Pepper's Lonely Hearts Club
  Band* (Beatles), 85–86, 87, 126
Sex, 19–20
"Sexy Ways" (H. Ballard), 19
Simon, Carly, 121
Simon, Paul, 97–98; "Bridge Over
  Troubled Waters," 97
Simon and Garfunkel, 97, 126
Sinatra, Frank, 35
"Shake, Rattle and Roll" (Bill Ha-
  ley), 17
Shaw, Sandi, 118
"Sh-Boom," 20; Chords', 16–17;
  Crew Cuts', 17
"She Loves You" (Beatles), 34
Shirelles, 118
Shrimpton, Jean, 41, 42
Skiffle, 33
Slade, 134
Slick, Grace, 117, 119
Small Faces, 98
"Space Oddity" (Bowie), 136
Spencer Davis Group, 95;
  "Gimme Some Lovin'," 56
Soft Machine, 96
"Stairway to Heaven" (Led Zep-
  pelin), 93
Stand Up (Jethro Tull), 101
Starr, Ringo, 37, 107, 137

Steele, Tommy, 33
Stephen, John, 41
Stewart, Rod, 98
Sticky Fingers (Stones), 99
Stoller, Mike, 125
"Strawberry Fields" (Beatles), 126
"Sunshine of Your Love" (Cream), 88
Supergroups, 57
Surfaris: "Wipe Out," 68
"Surf City" (Jan and Dean), 68
"Surfer Bird" (Rivingtons), 31
"Surfer Girl" (Beach Boys), 68
Surfing music, 32
"Surfin' Surfari" (Beach Boys), 68
"Surfin' USA" (Beach Boys), 68
"Suzie Q" (Hawkins/Creedance Clearwater), 95
Swan Song Records, 115
Sweet, 134

Tapestry (King), 119
Taupin, Bernie, 137
Taylor, James, 115
Technology, 121–27
Techno Rock, 91
Teddy Bears, 118
Television, 4–7
Their Satanic Majesties Request (Stones), 85, 87, 99
Thick As A Brick (Jethro Tull), 101
Thomas, Carla, 118
Thomas, Rufus: "Walking the Dog," 31–32
"Til There Was You" (Wilson/Beatles), 36
Tin Pan Alley, 16
"Toad" (Cream), 57
"Tom Dooley" (Kingston Trio), 63
Tommy (Who), 99–100
Tornadoes, 33
Townshend, Pete, 53, 54, 100
Traffic, 96
T. Rex, 135
"Two Faces Have I" (Lew Christie), 31

Vanilla Fudge, 99
Vee, Bobby, 106
Vietnam, 76, 78, 93

Wakeman, Rick, 124
"Walking the Dog" (Rufus Thomas), 31–32
Warner Communications, 115
Warner-Reprise Records, 115
Waters, Muddy, 47
Watkins, Peter, 35
Watts, Charlie, 50, 107. *See also* Rolling Stones
Weathermen, 78
Weber, Andrew Lloyd, 100
West Coast scene, 67, 101, 107–8. *See also* California
Wheels of Fire (Cream), 91
Who, The, 38, 43, 53–55, 57, 78, 86, 92, 99–100; "My Generation," 54; *Tommy*, 99–100; *Who's Next*, 100
Who's Next (Who), 100
Wild One, The, 18
Williamson, Sonny Boy, 56
Wilson, Dennis, 70
Wings: *Band on the Run*, 137
Winwood, Stevie, 56, 95
"Wipe Out" (Surfaris), 68
Witch and Warlock Rock, 91
Woodstock Art and Music Festival, 78–79, 94
Woodstock Nation, 78–79, 83
"Work with Me, Annie" (H. Ballard), 19
Wyman, Bill, 50. *See also* Rolling Stones

Yardbirds, 48, 55–56, 91–92; "For Your Love," 56; "I'm a Man," 56; "Over Under Sideways Down," 56
Yes, 124
"Your Cash Ain't Nothin' But Trash," 20